T0109656

THE PASTOR

GEOFFREY CHANG

THE **PASTOR**

RECOVERING A
BIBLICAL & THEOLOGICAL
VISION FOR MINISTRY

B&H
PUBLISHING
BRENTWOOD, TENNESSEE

Copyright © 2022 by Geoffrey Chang
All rights reserved.
Printing in the United States of America

978-1-0877-4784-2

Published by B&H Publishing Group
Brentwood, Tennessee

Dewey Decimal Classification: 253.7
Subject Heading: SPURGEON, C.H. / PASTORAL
THEOLOGY / MINISTRY

Unless otherwise noted, all Scripture quotations are
taken from the Christian Standard Bible®, Copyright ©
2017 by Holman Bible Publishers. Used by permission.
Christian Standard Bible® and CSB® are federally registered
trademarks of Holman Bible Publishers.

Also used: King James Version (KJV), public domain.

Book cover photo © National Portrait Gallery, London.
Author photo © Kaden Classen. Historical illustration from
Life and Works of Rev. Charles H. Spurgeon, Public domain.

2 3 4 5 6 7 8 • 27 26 25 24 23

To pastors called by God to shepherd His flock.
(1 Peter 5:1–4)

CONTENTS

ABBREVIATIONS

AARM—An All-Round Ministry: Addresses to Ministers and Students. London: Passmore & Alabaster, 1900.

Autobiography—C. H. Spurgeon's Autobiography: Compiled from His Diary, Letters, and Records, by His Wife, and His Private Secretary. Vols. 1–4. London: Passmore & Alabaster, 1897.

GFW—The Greatest Fight in the World: Conference Address. London: Passmore & Alabaster, 1895.

Lectures—Lectures to My Students: Addresses Delivered to the Students of the Pastor's College. Vols. 1–4. London: Passmore & Alabaster, 1881–1894.

LS—The Lost Sermons of C. H. Spurgeon. Vols. 1–6 Eds. Christian George, Jason Duesing, and Geoffrey Chang. Nashville: B&H Academic, 2016–2021.

MTP—The Metropolitan Tabernacle Pulpit: Sermons Preached and Revised by C. H. Spurgeon. Vols. 7–63. Pasadena, TX: Pilgrim Publications, 1970–2006.

NPSP—The New Park Street Pulpit: Containing Sermons Preached and Revised by the Rev. C. H. Spurgeon, Minister of the Chapel. Vols. 1–6. Pasadena, TX: Pilgrim Publications, 1975–1991.

S&T—The Sword and the Trowel; A Record of Combat with Sin & Labour for the Lord. 37 vols. London: Passmore & Alabaster, 1865–1902.

TD—The Treasury of David: Containing an Original Exposition of the Book of Psalms; A Collection of Illustrative Extracts from the Whole Range of Literature; A Series of Homiletical Hints Upon Almost Every Verse; And Lists of Writers Upon Each Psalm. 7 vols. London: Passmore & Alabaster, 1869–1885.

ANOTHER FORGOTTEN
SPURGEON

The Beginning of My Spurgeon Studies

Sometimes, life is changed by a major decision or event. For me, it was changed by an email. In 2016, I was happily serving as an associate pastor at Hinson Baptist Church in Portland, Oregon. I had been there since 2010 and in God's kindness, the church was healthy. So, wanting to further my pastoral training, I decided to pursue doctoral studies at Midwestern Baptist Theological Seminary in Kansas City, Missouri. After being accepted, I emailed my former pastor, Mark Dever, to ask for guidance on a dissertation topic. In classic fashion, he responded: "Something on Spurgeon's ecclesiology!!! Guaranteed edification!"

That short email led me to studying the ecclesiology of the most famous preacher of the nineteenth century. It led me to the archives of the Metropolitan Tabernacle, London, to the records of the Angus Library at Regent's Park, Oxford, to the offices of Pilgrim Publications in Pasadena, Texas, to out-of-the-way Spurgeon collections across America, and, of course, to many long nights exploring Spurgeon's own books housed in the Spurgeon Library in Kansas City. Ultimately, that email led to a whole new career in Spurgeon scholarship.

Today, I have the privilege of teaching at Midwestern Seminary and managing the Spurgeon Library. Midwestern exists to train up pastors and ministers who are committed to serving the local church. There is no better model of faithful pastoral ministry and commitment to the local church than Charles Haddon Spurgeon.

Another Forgotten Spurgeon

One of the surprising discoveries of my research was how overlooked Spurgeon's pastoral ministry has been over the years. This doesn't mean that Spurgeon himself has been overlooked. Arnold Dallimore estimates that in the years following his death, a new biography was published every month.[1] While his popularity declined in the United Kingdom in the years after his death, Spurgeon has remained as popular as ever in the United States and other parts of the world. To this day, his works are still translated, and every Sunday, his sermons are quoted from pulpits around the world. And since the middle of the twentieth century, academic works have been produced critically examining Spurgeon's life and teaching. These works have not only sought to take Spurgeon seriously as a preacher, but as a theologian. With the establishment of the Spurgeon Library in 2015, a new wave of Spurgeon scholarship has begun, seeking to organize his theology and discern his impact during his lifetime and beyond.

In 1966, Iain Murray published *The Forgotten Spurgeon*, where he writes, "Despite the modern encomiums bestowed on him as 'the prince of preachers' and despite the anecdotes which still survive in the evangelical world about his abilities and his humor, some of

---

[1] Arnold Dallimore, *Spurgeon: A New Biography* (Edinburgh: The Banner of Truth Trust, 1999), ix. These biographies were written mostly by his associates and friends. While they provided some new insights and anecdotes, they largely covered familiar territory.

the most important aspects of his ministry have been forgotten."[2] In his work, Murray argues that it is Spurgeon's theological framework that has been forgotten, "and Spurgeon without his theology is about as distorted as the cheap china figures of Spurgeon which were offered for sale by charlatans more than a century ago."[3]

Murray explores Spurgeon's theology through the various theological controversies that he encountered throughout his life. Those battles highlight Spurgeon's evangelical orthodoxy, particularly as it relates to his doctrine of Scripture, sin, the person and work of Christ, and salvation. Much of the renewed interest in Spurgeon's theology focuses on these doctrines. Still, little attention has been given to his understanding of the church. Spurgeon's ecclesiology and pastoral ministry remain a part of the forgotten Spurgeon.

Though many have told the stories from Spurgeon's background, preaching ministry, publications, orphanage, controversies, and more, very few have sought to examine the foundation of his ministry, namely his pastoring of a local church. Ever since the fall of 1851, when he was called as the bi-vocational pastor of the Baptist congregation in Waterbeach, Spurgeon's ministry was rooted in the local church. Some historians have noted how Spurgeon's ministry exemplified the fourfold evangelical emphasis of biblicism, crucicentrism, conversionism, and activism.[4] To those four, I would add a fifth (to invent a word): ecclesialcentrism.

Drawing on the Reformed tradition, which was sharpened by Baptist convictions, Spurgeon believed that Christian discipleship was rooted in and shaped by the local church. Along with all his other biblical and theological convictions, Spurgeon also had convictions about the local church. Biblical authority ruled the church, and

---

[2] Iain Murray, *The Forgotten Spurgeon* (Edinburgh: The Banner of Truth Trust, 2002), 4.

[3] Ibid., 5.

[4] See D. W. Bebbington, *Evangelicalism in Modern Britain: A History from the 1730s to the 1980s* (London: Routledge, 2000), 2–17.

was exercised by the congregation, under the leadership of elders and deacons. The message of the cross was to be proclaimed from the church for the conversion of sinners. Those who experienced conversion would publicly profess their faith through baptism and membership in the church. The church was also to be an engine for evangelistic and social activism. For Spurgeon, the church was not optional to the Christian life. It was the place in which the Christian life was to be lived out. This was the vision he sought to implement in his own church and promote in his pastoral training.

Some scholars have observed Spurgeon's love for his fellow evangelicals and his eagerness to cooperate with them. As a result, they have concluded that Spurgeon minimized his own ecclesiological convictions. But this does not give a full picture. Yes, Spurgeon gladly cooperated outside of his denomination. However, the aim of his preaching, evangelism, pastoral training, and church planting was not simply to promote evangelical doctrine, but to plant distinctly Baptist churches.

One of the main instruments for organizing this work was his monthly magazine, *The Sword and the Trowel*. Writing in the very first article of the magazine in 1865, Spurgeon declared that his goal was "to advocate those views of doctrine *and Church order* which are most certainly received among us."[5] For more than twenty-five years, this magazine provided not only Spurgeon's gospel teaching, but also, as Tom Nettles notes, his "view of pastoral ministry . . . [and] his views on the life of the church."[6] Spurgeon's convictions about pastoral ministry and the church even led him to spread his views beyond his own congregation to the rest of the English-speaking world.

---

[5] *S&T* 1865:1.

[6] Tom Nettles, *Living by Revealed Truth: The Life and Pastoral Theology of Charles Haddon Spurgeon* (Ross-shire: Christian Focus, 2013), 9.

Drawing on primary sources like *The Sword and the Trowel*, his sermons, church minutes, and more, this book will seek to bring out this overlooked theme of Spurgeon's life. We will focus particularly on Spurgeon's pastoral ecclesiology, looking at topics like the role of preaching in the church, corporate gatherings, membership interviews, elders and deacons, and much more.[7] My main argument will be that Spurgeon's approach to these church matters was driven by biblical and theological convictions, rather than by pragmatism or convenience. For this reason, he remains a valuable conversation partner for pastors today.

Why Listen to Spurgeon?

Why should pastors care about Spurgeon's thoughts on the church? Let me offer three reasons:

1. Spurgeon pastored amid an active ministry. His sixty-three volumes of published sermons make it clear that the heart of Spurgeon's ministry was preaching, and this kept him busy. From his earliest days at Waterbeach, he would regularly preach eight times a week (three sermons on Sunday and five nights a week). After a few years in London, the demand for his preaching was so great that he found himself preaching as much as twelve or thirteen times a week.[8] But as busy as Spurgeon was, he was more than just a preacher. He gave oversight to at least sixty-six institutions that existed out of the Metropolitan Tabernacle, including two orphanages, the Pastors' College, numerous Bible classes, Sunday schools, and more. We also can't forget the incessant deadlines of his weekly sermon publications, monthly magazine, unending correspondence,

---

[7] For a study of Spurgeon's ecclesiology proper, see my forthcoming work, *The Army of God: Spurgeon's Vision for the Church* (Ross-shire: Christian Focus, 2022).

[8] *Autobiography* 2:81.

and many book projects. But as important and fruitful as those ministries were, Spurgeon was more than just a ministry director and administrator. Spurgeon was a pastor. He took responsibility for a church and sought to care for his flock. Busy-ness was no excuse to neglect his pastoral responsibilities.

So, why should we listen to Spurgeon? For the church leader with thousands of responsibilities, we need Spurgeon to remind us of the importance of our calling as pastors and to encourage us to persevere in faithfulness.

2. Spurgeon pastored amid a revival. When Spurgeon first arrived in London, the congregation of the New Park Street Chapel had dwindled to a few dozen. Sitting in a cavernous building that seated over a thousand, Spurgeon may have thought he had plenty of room to expand. But in just a few months, the whole city was stirred at the news of the boy-preacher from the fens. The roads and bridges leading to Spurgeon's chapel were blocked by traffic each Sunday. Before long, the congregation outgrew their space and needed to expand. During construction, Spurgeon rented large venues, like Exeter Hall and the Surrey Gardens Music Hall, to accommodate the growing crowds, but hundreds were still being turned away. And as the building expansion finished, the congregation once again outgrew their space.

The challenge of space vexed Spurgeon. But this wasn't about drawing the largest crowd possible. Instead, this was Spurgeon's recognition that he was the pastor of a church, not an itinerant preacher. At one point, he lamented how membership had exceeded the seating at the New Park Street Chapel by 300, which meant that if they were to observe the Lord's Supper in their building, 300 members would not be able to participate. Not only that but with so many being converted, Spurgeon feared that he could not responsibly bring them into church membership and care for them properly. The only options he could think of was to either build a larger building or quit the pastorate altogether and become a traveling evangelist. But his congregation did not let him quit. They would approve the construction of a new building, seating well over 5,000. Even as church membership grew from 50 to 5,000, Spurgeon's view of pastoral ministry remained the same.

Why should we listen to Spurgeon? For pastors of large churches who are tempted to compromise their ecclesiology, Spurgeon offers an example of faithfulness even amid rapid growth.

3. Spurgeon pastored amid numerous societal and theological challenges. As the most famous pastor of the English-speaking world, people wanted Spurgeon's opinions on everything. Living in London during the Victorian era at the height of British imperialism, there were no shortage of societal and theological issues to discuss. From Darwinism to American slavery, from cholera outbreaks to the industrial revolution, from international wars to the temperance movement, from women's suffrage to state religion, and much, much more, Spurgeon had plenty to distract him from his pastoral ministry. To be clear, Spurgeon commented on many of these issues through his magazine and public correspondence, sometimes at great cost to himself. Still, Spurgeon understood that he was not responsible for pastoring the entire English-speaking world. His responsibility lay with the members of the Metropolitan Tabernacle. Even as Spurgeon engaged prophetically in the world around him, he never lost sight that his responsibility was for the members of his local church.

Why should we listen to Spurgeon? Even as we face controversies in our day, Spurgeon provides a model for faithfully pastoring our congregations through those challenges.

A Word of Caution

I once heard of a Spurgeon enthusiast at a Baptist convention selling vials of water from the River Lark (the river where Spurgeon was baptized . . . a Baptist version of the Jordan River, if you will). As the story goes, at least one person bought a vial and sprinkled some of that water on himself to help him with his preaching! In case any are tempted toward this kind of Spurgeonic superstition, let me offer a word of advice about how to use this book.

This book is not about techniques for how to "do church" just like Spurgeon did. There is no guarantee that if you do these things, you will see the same kind of revival that Spurgeon saw. In fact, these practices may lead to decline before they lead to any growth. If you try to imitate Spurgeon without careful teaching and consideration of your context, you may very well get fired! Consider yourself warned.

My argument is that Spurgeon pastored out of biblical and theological convictions. When we consider Spurgeon's pastoral practice, we must understand that behind those practices are convictions about the nature of the church and pastoral ministry. At the heart of his pastoral strategy was the belief that the Bible is sufficient and speaks to how the church is to be led. So, the best way to think about this book is as a conversation partner to help you consider what faithfulness in ministry looks like. Here is how one pastor sought to faithfully apply his convictions, given his church context. As you read, consider your own context. Examine your convictions from Scripture about the church and pastoral ministry. And pray about what it might look like to pursue faithfulness in your ministry.

Layout

We begin with the church gathered for worship (chapters 1–2). In the first chapter, we will be looking not so much at Spurgeon's approach to preaching (though we will deal with some of that), but more importantly, the role of preaching in the life of the church.

Chapter 2 will discuss more broadly the corporate worship of the Metropolitan Tabernacle. How did Spurgeon organize the worship services? What was his approach to congregational singing? And so on.

Having gathered for worship and been shaped by God's Word, now the church begins to take shape. The next section (chapters 3–5) addresses the constitution of the church. The ordinances of baptism and the Lord's Supper play a big role in Spurgeon's understanding of the church, and chapter 3 will explore their significance. Chapter 4 will deal with church membership and how people were brought into the church. But more than simply having a large membership roll, Spurgeon wanted to have meaningful membership, where church members were known and engaged and cared for. Chapter 5 will explain how Spurgeon did that in a church of 5,000.

Having properly drawn the boundaries of membership, Spurgeon did not envision the church as a headless body. Rather, he had clear convictions about the leadership and structure of the church, and this will be addressed in the following section (chapters 6–7). Chapter 6 will discuss Spurgeon's view of the roles and responsibilities of church officers, namely pastors, elders, and deacons. Apart from their tireless labors alongside him, Spurgeon believed that the church would have a been a complete sham. It was their spiritual and practical service that made the Metropolitan Tabernacle possible. Spurgeon was also a congregationalist. The leadership of the elders existed alongside the authority of the congregation. Chapter 7 will explore how Spurgeon implemented congregationalism even as the church grew exponentially.

Finally, the church was made alive by God's Word. The next section (chapters 8–9) sees the church ready to engage the world with the gospel. For Spurgeon, the church was not a country club. It was an army amid a spiritual battle. And so, he called his members to engage in the fight. As great as Spurgeon's impact was, that is only one part of the story. Out of the Metropolitan Tabernacle came countless gospel endeavors. Their full impact will only be known in eternity. Chapter 8 addresses the many charitable and evangelistic institutions that were established out of the Tabernacle and chapter 9 will deal with Spurgeon's approach to pastoral training and church planting. Chapter 10 will then offer some brief concluding thoughts.

Preaching in 1870, Spurgeon declared,

> The proper study of the Christian is Christ. Next to that subject is the Church. And though I would by no means ever urge you so to think of the Church as for a moment to put her in comparison with her Lord yet think of her in relation to him. You will not dishonor the sun by remembering that there is a moon, you will not lessen the glory of "the King in his beauty" by remembering that the Queen, his Consort, is "all glorious within." You will not think any the less of Christ for thinking much of his Church.[9]

Spurgeon's love for Christ prompted him to also love the church. And as he encouraged his people to think rightly about the church, he believed this would only increase their love of Christ. My prayer is that our study of the church and pastoral ministry through Spurgeon's ministry would have the same effect on us; that we would not think any less of Christ for thinking much of His Church, but instead, we would be ever more devoted to Christ and to His people.

---

[9] *MTP* 60:433.

1

THE THERMOPYLAE
OF THE CHURCH

PREACHING

The Prince of Preachers

The numbers associated with Spurgeon's preaching ministry are staggering. He began preaching at the age of sixteen. By the time he was called to be the pastor of the New Park Street Chapel at the age of nineteen, he had composed 365 sermons and preached nearly 700 times. In his more than thirty-eight years of ministry in London, Spurgeon preached anywhere from four to thirteen times a week. He preached when he was away on vacation. He preached when he was sick (at times, he had to be carried down from the pulpit). If he was unable to preach at the Tabernacle due to illness or travel, he would often provide a written sermon to be read for Sunday worship. We cannot know how many sermons he preached over his lifetime, but a conservative estimate might be around 10,000.

Beginning in 1855, his sermons were published and sold in weekly pamphlets called "The Penny Pulpit," with an average circulation of 25,000, but in one case, selling as many as 350,000 copies. Because his sermons were so popular, he couldn't just recycle an old sermon when preaching away. He often brought a new one. At the end of each year, his weekly sermons were collected in the *New*

Park Street Pulpit and the *Metropolitan Tabernacle Pulpit* volumes. After his death in 1892, the series would continue for over two decades, ending only in 1917 because of a paper shortage from the war. In all, 3,563 sermons were published in sixty-three volumes, with more left unpublished. These sermons were sold throughout the English-speaking world and were translated into nearly forty languages. Spurgeon's publishers estimated that more than 100 million sermons were sold.

All these astounding numbers confirm that Spurgeon's mission in life was to preach. If we are to understand Spurgeon's view of pastoral ministry, we must begin with the pulpit. Spurgeon believed that God builds His church through His Word. Therefore, preaching is at the heart of pastoral ministry. This chapter will explore the role of preaching in Spurgeon's pastoral ministry, first by examining the relationship of preaching and the church, and then by considering Spurgeon's approach to preaching.

A Life Changed by Preaching

Where did Spurgeon's commitment to preaching come from? To understand the Prince of Preachers, it's important to recognize that he not only gave himself *to* preaching, but he himself was radically changed *by* preaching.

Growing up in a pastor's home, Spurgeon gained an interest in spiritual matters at a young age. The discipline of his father and grandfather kept him out of trouble, and the teaching of his mother deeply impacted him. Even so, beneath his religious, church-going exterior, Spurgeon knew the sin of his heart. Between the ages of ten and fifteen, Spurgeon struggled with doubts, discouragement, and the guilt of his sin. As a result, he fell into despair. At one point, he even experimented with atheism and skepticism, but when he saw the void of "the nothingness of vacuity," he turned back. For years, he sought relief in the Puritan works in his grandfather's library, by going to church, by being active in religious societies, by refraining from worldly activities, and more. But none of these relieved his guilty conscience. All the while, Spurgeon wondered, "What must I do to be saved?"

The answer came during the Christmas break of 1849–1850. Fifteen-year-old Spurgeon was home from school, in Colchester. While hoping to find the way of salvation, he decided to visit every place of worship in town that winter. On Sunday morning, January 6, 1850, on his way to another church, a sudden snowstorm forced Spurgeon to turn in to the Artillery Street Primitive Methodist chapel, with a dozen or so people in attendance. The regular minister was unable to make it, so an unknown lay deacon took his place and preached on Isaiah 45:22, "Look unto me, and be ye saved, all the ends of the earth" (KJV). He was not eloquent or well-educated. But he preached clearly about what it meant to respond to the gospel.

> Just fixing his eyes on me, as if he knew all my heart, he said, "Young man, you look very miserable." Well, I did; but I had not been accustomed to have remarks made from the pulpit on my personal appearance before. However, it was a good blow, struck right home. He continued, "and you always will be miserable—miserable in life, and miserable in death,—if you don't obey my text; but if you obey now, this moment, you will be saved." Then, lifting up his hands, he shouted, as only a Primitive Methodist could do, "Young man, look to Jesus Christ. Look! Look! Look! You have nothin' to do but to look and live."[1]

---

[1] *Autobiography* 1:106.

For years, Spurgeon had known about Christ's death on the cross for sinners, but he had never understood what was required of him. Preachers normally emphasized God's power and the need to prove one's faith by acting like a Christian. But now, sitting there in the pew, dripping wet, Spurgeon understood for the first time that faith was not doing anything for Christ but looking to Christ as your all-sufficient Savior.[2]

The unique circumstances of Spurgeon's conversion would forever leave a mark on his subsequent ministry. Spurgeon never got over the fact that he was converted under the preaching of the Word.

> Personally, I have to bless God for many good books . . . but my gratitude most of all is due to God, not for books, but for the preached Word. . . . The books were good, but the man was better. The revealed Word awakened me; but it was the preached Word that saved me; and I must ever attach peculiar value to the hearing of the truth, for by it I received the joy and peace in which my soul delights.[3]

Spurgeon understood that preaching was only the medium. The substance and power of preaching lay in "the revealed Word," the gospel, not in the preacher himself. This understanding was underscored by the fact that this sermon came from a poor, uneducated man with no training, who barely got through the sermon.

---

[2] "I had been waiting to do fifty things, but when I heard that word, 'Look!' what a charming word it seemed to me! Oh! I looked until I could almost have looked my eyes away. There and then the cloud was gone, the darkness had rolled away, and that moment I saw the sun; and I could have risen that instant, and sung with the most enthusiastic of them, of the precious blood of Christ, and the simple faith which looks alone to Him." *Autobiography* 1:106.

[3] *Autobiography* 1:104.

Throughout his ministry, Spurgeon was not afraid to use other mediums to communicate the gospel, and he gave himself to writing books, organizing Sunday schools, encouraging private devotions, equipping his people for evangelism, and more.

But because of his experience, he always believed there was a "peculiar value" in the preaching and hearing of the Word. Something unique takes place when the Word "comes with a living power from living lips."[4] As he states in the Preface of his first volume of sermons, "The Preaching of the Word by the chosen servants of the living God, is the ordained means for the gathering in of the elect."[5] It was this conviction that he carried with him into pastoral ministry.

The Thermopylae of the Church

As the rest of this book will show, Spurgeon's pastoral ministry was more than just preaching. With so much to do, he envied Daniel Rowland who "would have nothing to do with the management of the church. . . . He kept himself to his preaching, came in through a door in the back wall of the meeting-house and disappeared suddenly when he had done." A pastor in that situation "ought to preach like an angel."[6] This was not Spurgeon's situation. He did not occupy a preaching station but pastored a church.

And yet, we should note that Spurgeon's pastoral ministry was not less than preaching. Even with everything on his plate, he never failed in this most fundamental of pastoral responsibilities: to preach the Word. Spurgeon believed this to be true not only for himself but for all pastors. Spurgeon believed that the pulpit was "the Thermopylae of Christendom." But in referring to "Christendom,"

---

[4] *MTP* 53:188.
[5] *NPSP* 1: Preface.
[6] *S&T* 1886:83.

Spurgeon did not have any grand ideas about a Christian nation. Rather, he was referring to the local church. Just as the future of Greece depended on King Leonidas I in the Battle of Thermopylae, so Spurgeon believed that the health and unity of the church depended on the preaching of the Word. No matter how industrious of an administrator or counselor a pastor was, if he failed in his preaching, the church would also fail. At the pulpit, "the fight will be lost or won." Therefore, Spurgeon charged his pastoral students that "the maintenance of our power in the pulpit should be our great concern, we must occupy that spiritual watch-tower with our hearts and minds awake and in full vigor."[7]

Throughout Spurgeon's ministry, for a congregation of more than 5,000 members, the Metropolitan Tabernacle demonstrated remarkable unity. The church meeting minutes do not give any evidence of congregational infighting or disagreement with the elders. The church repeatedly affirmed their love and support for their pastor. The reason for this cannot be that Spurgeon always made the right decisions and pastored his church perfectly. Rather, if you were to ask him, Spurgeon would point to his preaching. Week after week, his congregation was "really fed" from God's Word, and thus, they were satisfied and forgave "a great many sins." Therefore, for the pastor, "pulpits must be our main care," or everything else will fail.[8]

As we will see, Spurgeon's responsibilities as a pastor grew throughout his ministry. To help him with new members and pastoral care, Spurgeon led the church in calling men to serve as elders.

---

[7] *Lectures* 2:146.

[8] "We shall be forgiven a great many sins in the matter of pastoral visitation if the people's souls are really fed on the Sabbath-day; but fed they must be, and nothing else will make up for it. The failures of most ministers who drift down the stream may be traced to inefficiency in the pulpit. The chief business of a captain is to know how to handle his vessel, nothing can compensate for deficiency there, and so our pulpits must be our main care, or all will go awry." *Lectures* 2:146.

To help him with the day-to-day pastoral and administrative responsibilities, he brought on his brother, James, to serve as his associate
pastor. For all the various institutions and societies connected with
the church, he relied on his deacons to assist him in his leadership.

But when it came to the pulpit ministry of the church, Spurgeon
alone took charge of the responsibility. He did most of the preaching, and when he was unable to preach, he arranged for pulpit supply from faithful preachers. This is not because he was territorial
about the pulpit. Rather, Spurgeon understood that the heart of
his pastoral calling was to responsibly give oversight to the preaching of the Word. The health and ministry of the church depended
on this one thing, and he would not delegate that responsibility to
anyone else.

As a result, Spurgeon felt the weight of responsibility in his
preaching. The pulpit was his Thermopylae, and every sermon was
a spiritual battle against the schemes of Satan. Because he preached
so often and was so gifted, it would be easy to imagine Spurgeon
growing comfortable with the task of preaching. This, however, was
far from the case. Susannah, his wife, tells of the "soul-travail and
spiritual anguish" that Spurgeon experienced during his sermon
writing, not "in their preparation or arrangement, but in his own
sense of accountability to God for the souls to whom he had to preach
the gospel of salvation."[9] As his congregation multiplied and his
sermons were being published around the world, Spurgeon felt the
growing responsibility of each sermon. One friend tells how, in his
earlier years, Spurgeon could not keep anything down before each
sermon, in anticipation of the throngs who would gather to hear
him. Only later in life would that physical struggle be overcome.

He did not, however, find this to be a deficiency. He once confessed to his grandfather about his physical and emotional struggles

---

[9] *Autobiography* 4:65.

before entering the pulpit. His grandfather responded, "Be content to have it so; for when your emotion goes away your strength will be gone." Though he preached thousands of sermons, Spurgeon never got over the weighty and awesome responsibility of preaching. "When we preach and think nothing of it, the people think nothing of it, and God does nothing by it."[10] As his ministry grew, Spurgeon did not coast in the pulpit but approached each sermon with trembling and prayerful dependence. This was his work as a pastor.

Preaching Shapes the Church

Spurgeon taught that a pastor who fed his congregation from God's Word would go a long way in keeping the church united and happy under his leadership. Spurgeon believed that preaching shapes the church. Preaching is how a pastor leads and grows the church spiritually. The character and health of the church depend on the ministry of the Word. Therefore, the strongest influence for spiritual growth in the church lay not with the elders or deacons or Sunday school teachers but with the preacher. "Doubtless the hearers influence the preacher, but for the most part the stronger current runs the other way."[11]

Spurgeon saw many negative examples of this principle in the churches of his day. Many of these churches had a historic ministry. But over the years, new pastors came in with modern theologies and new emphases. Inevitably, the pulpit was no longer central in these churches and what preaching remained was characterized

---

[10] S&T 1882:406.

[11] "No one can doubt that the spiritual condition of the Christian church is very much affected by the character of its ministry. For good or for evil, the leaders do actually lead to a very large extent. Doubtless the hearers influence the preacher, but for the most part the stronger current runs the other way. 'Like priest, like people,' is a well-known and truthful proverb, applicable with undiminished force to those who scorn the priestly title." S&T 1871:215.

more by intellectualism and current events, rather than the gospel. As a result, these churches began to wither spiritually. Prayer meetings were canceled. Evangelistic fervor declined. Worldly entertainments crept into the church. Such churches might attract people with their innovations, but Spurgeon saw that the spiritual condition had changed. In all these things, he traced the root of these problems to the pulpit.[12]

The solution, then, was to reform the pulpit and help churches see the importance of the faithful preaching of God's Word. Spurgeon rejected those who undermined the pastorate and "would pull down the men God has raised up." Rather, he believed that the pulpit was at the heart of the life of the church. A faithful ministry of the Word is "the instrumentality by which the Lord especially works" in the church. Churches that rejected "God's chosen instrumentality of ministry" would soon have "Ichabod!" written upon their walls.[13] But through the ministry of the Word, God displays His power in the church and in the world.

Therefore, as we'll see in chapter 9, Spurgeon devoted himself to raising up faithful preachers of God's Word. He could not envision reforming any church apart from the pulpit. Apart from the power of God's Word, any efforts at church reform would fail. But if a dying church would call a faithful preacher to fill the pulpit and preach God's Word faithfully, Spurgeon believed, by God's grace, that any church could be restored and once again see God's blessing upon its ministry.

---

[12] "Under a drowsy preacher the spirit of the people becomes lethargic; a minister absorbed in politics leads his hearers into party strifes; a would-be intellectual essayist breeds a discipleship marked by affectation of superior culture; and an unsound thinker and uncertain talker promotes heresy in his congregation. Satan knows full well the power of the ministry, and therefore he labors abundantly to pervert the minds of the Lord's servants, and also to raise up false teachers who may do his evil cause great service." *S&T* 1871:215.

[13] *MTP* 8:196.

Spurgeon's Approach to Preaching

If you are looking to grow in your preaching, let me commend Spurgeon's instructions on preaching to you, found in *Lectures to My Students*. At least twenty out of the thirty-two published lectures deal directly with preaching, giving practical teaching, as well as a theological vision for preaching. For the purposes of this book, allow me to highlight seven brief points to summarize Spurgeon's approach to preaching. If you are a regular preacher yourself, perhaps you will find something in Spurgeon's example to encourage you in your labors.

Prepared

Having preached thousands of sermons, when did Spurgeon ever find time to prepare them? One answer is that Spurgeon never really stopped preparing. He was always thinking about his sermons, meditating on Scripture, on the lookout for good content, and, in general, working on his craft as a preacher. Spurgeon warned his students, "We ought to be always in training for text-getting and sermon-making . . . the leaf of your ministry will soon wither unless, like the blessed man in the first Psalm, you meditate in the law of the Lord both day and night . . . I have no belief in that ministry which ignores laborious preparation."[14]

Sermon preparation not only focused on the manuscript, but also the preacher himself. Spurgeon reminded his students that preachers are "our own tools, and therefore must keep ourselves in order."[15] This included not only cultivating the right skills and abilities, but it also meant keeping one's heart and soul in nearness to Christ and love for the lost. Such preparations did begin and end in the study but marked the preacher's entire life.

---

[14] *Lectures* 1:97.
[15] *Lectures* 1:1.

More specifically, however, Spurgeon did have a sermon preparation process that usually took place on Saturday evenings after 6:00 p.m. He once gave the following description of his process:

Brethren, it is not easy for me to tell you precisely how I make my sermons. All through the week I am on the look-out for material that I can use on the Sabbath; but the actual work of arranging it is necessarily, left until Saturday evening, for every other moment is fully occupied in the Lord's service. I have often said that my greatest difficulty is to fix my mind upon the particular texts which are to be the subjects of discourse, on the following day; or, to speak more correctly, to know what topics the Holy Spirit would have me bring before the congregation. As soon as any passage of Scripture really grips my heart and soul, I concentrate my whole attention upon it, look at the precise meaning of the original, closely examine the context so as to see the special aspect of the text in its surroundings, and roughly jot down all the thoughts that occur to me concerning the subject, leaving to a later period the orderly marshalling of them for presentation to my hearers.

When I have reached this point, I am often stopped by an obstacle which is only a trouble to those of us whose sermons are regularly printed. I turn to my own Bible, which contains a complete record of all my published discourses; and, looking at these I have preached upon the text, I find, perhaps, that the general run of thought is so similar to that which I have marked out, that I have to abandon the subject, and seek another.

Happily, a text of Scripture is like a diamond with many facets, which sparkles and flashes whichever way it is held, so that, although I may have already printed, several sermons upon a particular passage, there is still a fresh setting possible for the priceless gem, and I can go forward with my work. I like next to see what others have to say about my text; and, as a rule, my experience is that, if its teaching is perfectly plain, the commentators, to a man, explain it at great length, whereas, with equal unanimity, they studiously avoid or evade the verses which Peter might have described as 'things hard to be understood.' I am very much obliged to them for leaving me so many nuts to crack; but I should have been just as grateful if they had made more use of their own theological teeth or nut-crackers. However, among the many who have written upon the Word, I generally find some who can at least help to throw a side light upon it; and when I have arrived at that part of my preparation, I am glad to call my dear wife to my assistance. She reads to me until I get a clear idea of the whole subject; and, gradually, I am guided to the best form of outline, which I copy out, on a half-sheet of notepaper, for use in the pulpit. This relates only to the morning sermon; for the evening, I am usually content if I can decide upon the text, and have a general notion of the lessons to be drawn from it, leaving to the Lord's-day afternoon the final arrangement of divisions, sub-divisions, and illustrations.[16]

Notice that Spurgeon does not commend this process as the best way to prepare a sermon. He acknowledges that his process is influenced by his unique circumstances and abilities. While he's glad to share his approach, each preacher must figure out what works best for him. Spurgeon's sermon prep process generally followed four steps.

First, he selected week-by-week the text from which he would preach. He found this to be "the greatest difficulty" of his preparations. This process involved not only careful study and pastoral consideration of his congregation's needs, but he also looked to the Spirit's leading. He shared with his students, "I confess that I frequently sit hour after hour praying and waiting for a subject, and that this is the main part of my study." But this was not a passive waiting. Even as he labored "in manipulating topics, ruminating upon points of doctrine, making skeletons out of verses," he depended on the Spirit to guide him to a text.[17] Spurgeon did not forbid his students from planning a sermon series ahead of time and preaching through books of the Bible. But he warned them that a long series could end up being wearisome to a congregation.[18] Part of the issue was that Spurgeon generally followed the Puritan model of preaching, which took one verse as its text and meditated on that text deeply. So, to preach through a book of the Bible one verse at a time could prove to be difficult, even for the most gifted of preachers.

Second, Spurgeon studied his text intensely, examining it in the original language, considering the surrounding context, and

---

[16] *Autobiography* 4:65–68.
[17] *Lectures* 1:88.
[18] *Lectures* 1:99–101.

jotting down all his thoughts and reflections on the text. Having done that work, he then went back to see if he had already preached on this text and compared his notes to make sure there was not too much overlap. Spurgeon believed Scripture to be "like a diamond with many facets" and thus, he often preached multiple sermons on a single verse. It must be said here that Spurgeon was remarkably original as a preacher of thousands of sermons. Some scholars have accused Spurgeon of being open to plagiarizing other's sermons. It is true that Spurgeon read widely and drew from others' insights, especially earlier in his preaching career. But it is clear that the heart of Spurgeon's sermon preparation was his original work and meditations on the text. He despised repeating himself, let alone another preacher.

Third, only *after* having studied it for himself, Spurgeon consulted other sources, both academic commentaries and devotional writings. He found academic works less useful in his preparation. He consulted them particularly for difficulties in the text, but too often, commentators evaded those difficulties. More helpful were devotional works and sermons. For this portion of his preparations, his wife read from selected works, while Spurgeon reflected on what he heard. Susannah was always amazed at her husband's knowledge of his library and cherished these times for her own spiritual growth.[19]

---

[19] "I always found, when I went into the study, an easy chair drawn up to the table, by his side, and a big heap of books piled one upon the other, and opened at the place where he desired me to read. With those old volumes around him, he was like a honeybee amid the flowers; he seemed to know how to extract and carry off the sweet spoils from the most unpromising-looking tome among them. His acquaintance with them was so familiar and complete, that he could at once place his hand on any author who had written upon the portion of Scripture which was engaging his attention; and I was, in this pleasant fashion, introduced to many of the Puritan and other divines whom, otherwise, I might not have known." *Autobiography* 4:68.

Finally, he took all he had studied, and he organized his sermon, writing down his thoughts onto a half-sheet of paper. Earlier in his preaching career, Spurgeon tended to write out his sermons in fuller outlines or even manuscripts. Some of the sermons found in the *Lost Sermons of C. H. Spurgeon* series can span several pages. But as he grew more experienced, Spurgeon forced himself to preach more extemporaneously, reducing his sermon preparation to a simple outline. This final step mattered because Spurgeon believed in the importance of well-arranged sermons. He taught his students that rather than simply letting truths fall at random from the pulpit, the sermon should proceed logically. "The thought must climb and ascend; one stair of teaching leading to another; one door of reasoning conducting to another, and the whole elevating the hearer to a chamber from whose windows truth is seen gleaming in the light of God."[20] Even though he only took an outline into the pulpit, it represented a disciplined process of preparation and prayer.

Extemporaneous

Spurgeon encouraged two kinds of extemporaneous preaching. The first was a sermon that was extemporaneous in its words, but not in content. These were the kinds of sermons he preached on Sunday mornings. Having carefully studied the text, organized his outline, and prepared his teaching points and illustrations, Spurgeon stepped into the pulpit fully prepared and at the same time relying on the Spirit to give him the right words to say.[21]

---

[20] *Lectures* 1:80.

[21] "Do not go into the pulpit and say the first thing that comes to hand, for the uppermost thing with most men is mere froth. Your people need discourses which have been prayed over and laboriously prepared. People do not want raw food, it must be cooked and made ready for them. We must give out of our very souls, in the words which naturally suggest themselves, the matter which has been as thoroughly prepared by us as it possibly could have been by a sermon-writer;

An extemporaneous delivery was extremely important to
Spurgeon. The last thing he wanted was for his sermon to sound
read. Sermon manuscripts were fine in preparation. Spurgeon
encouraged his students to write out their sermons and to revise
them carefully "that you may be preserved from a slipshod style."
But then after all that work is done, "leave them at home afterwards" and preach the sermon directly to the people. Spurgeon also
warned his students against memorizing sermons. This was "a wearisome exercise of an inferior power of the mind and an indolent
neglect of other and superior faculties." Instead, he commended
his own practice: "the words are extemporal, as I think they always
should be, but the thoughts are the result of research and study."[22]

Spurgeon also encouraged another kind of extemporaneous
preaching. For pastors who preached once or twice a week, they
could afford to spend the needed time preparing these sermons.
But for a busy pastor like Spurgeon who preached multiple times
a week, he had to develop a new skill. For his sermons on Monday
evenings, Spurgeon preached them almost entirely extemporaneously, exercising what he called "speech impromptu, without special preparation, without notes or immediate forethought." To be
sure, he warned against using this practice as the main diet of a
church's preaching. Such unstudied sermons tended to be of "a very
inferior quality," even from the most gifted of preachers. "Churches
are not to be held together except by an instructive ministry; a
mere filling up of time with oratory will not suffice."[23] Some traditions, like the Quakers, suffered because of their insistence on
impromptu preaching as the only method of preaching. Spurgeon

---

indeed, it should be even better prepared, if we would speak well. The best method
is, in my judgment, that in which the man does not extemporize the matter,
but extemporizes the words; the language comes to him at the moment, but the
theme has been well thought out." *Lectures* 1:142.

[22] *Lectures* 1:153.

[23] *Lectures* 1:151.

also warned about attempting this without practice. Such careless preaching would result in tiresome repetition, jumbled thoughts, and embarrassment.

At the same time, for the pastor who was disciplined in reading and meditation, who knew his congregation well, and who worked on this skill, such preaching could prove to be beneficial for the church and his own development as a preacher. Since his early days in London, Spurgeon sought "to get into the habit of speaking extemporaneously" by using the Monday night prayer meeting. Those meetings were smaller and more intimate, composed mostly of his own people. In those meetings, Spurgeon could afford to be more personal and speak from the heart.[24]

Just as any tradesman could speak about his work without any preparation, so should a preacher be able to expound on the doctrines of the gospel for the edification of his people. As Spurgeon developed this skill, he grew in his extemporaneous preaching on Sundays, and it equipped him for other impromptu preaching opportunities that he encountered.

Expositional

Spurgeon believed that the power of the pulpit lay not in the preacher, but in the Word of God. Therefore, he believed that preachers should preach expositional sermons. These were sermons that took a text of Scripture as their main theme and sought to explain and apply those texts to the people. Spurgeon did not forbid

---

[24] "I have never studied or prepared anything for the Monday evening prayer-meeting. I have all along selected that occasion as the opportunity for off-hand exhortation; but you will observe that I do not on such occasions select difficult expository topics, or abstruse themes, but restrict myself to simple, homely talk, about the elements of our faith. When standing up on such occasions, one's mind makes a review, and inquires, 'What subject has already taken up my thought during the day? What have I met with in my reading during the past week? What is most laid upon my heart at this hour? What is suggested by the hymns or the prayers?'" *Lectures* 1:158–159.

other kinds of sermons, but he charged pastors to make expositional preaching their main practice.[25]

When crafting a sermon, Spurgeon taught his students to stick closely to the text. Whatever doctrine or application they taught, their matter "must be congruous to the text." They should avoid thrusting the text to the side to make room for their own ideas. Instead, "the discourse should spring out of the text as a rule." This should be evident not only to the preacher but to all that listen. The more people can see that the preacher is speaking "plainly the very word of God," the more the sermon comes "with far greater power to the consciences of hearers."[26]

Some have critiqued Spurgeon's preaching and have wondered if he was really an expositional preacher. Perhaps in reading his devotions from *Morning and Evening* or working through one of his more typological sermons, some have found Spurgeon to be looser in his handling of the text than they're used to. At least two things can be said in response.

First, Spurgeon's expositional preaching was not about a style, but a commitment to rooting his sermons in the Word of God. Some associate expositional preaching with a certain style, particularly with verse-by-verse preaching. Spurgeon, however, cared less about style. He cared more about his preaching being rooted in God's Word. Preaching was "not a lecture about the Scripture, but Scripture itself opened up and enforced." Most of Spurgeon's sermons covered a single verse. But on occasion, he also preached longer passages (for example, see *MTP* 23, Sermon No. 1360, "The Good Samaritan," or *MTP* 55, Sermon No. 3155, "The Beatitudes").

---

[25] "Let us be mighty in expounding the Scriptures. I am sure that no preaching will last so long, or build up a church so well, as the expository. To renounce altogether the hortatory discourse for the expository, would be running to a preposterous extreme; but I cannot too earnestly assure you that, if your ministries are to be lastingly useful, you must be expositors." *AARM* 44.

[26] *Lectures* 1:75.

But regardless of style or length of passage, Spurgeon's aim (and the aim of all expositional preaching) was to open and apply the Scriptures to his people.

Second, Spurgeon was unafraid to preach the overarching narrative and theology of Scripture. When preaching on a single verse, Spurgeon often used that verse as a lens through which he meditated on all of Scripture, both systematically and redemptive-historically. But even in doing so, he did not abandon the text but constrained his reflections by it. Careful reading of his sermons will show that his points are not random; they are flowing from the structure and content of the passage. Additionally, Spurgeon was mindful of the context of the passage, which he often incorporated in the Scripture reading. In planning the service, Spurgeon always looked for readings drawn from the context or related to the text. He also provided brief commentary as he read so that by the sermon, his people had some understanding of the context. This preparatory work in the text allowed him to go further and deeper in his preaching without losing the historical-grammatical context.

At the end of the day, whether he succeeded in preaching any given sermon expositionally can be debated. What is clear is that Spurgeon advocated such preaching and sought to do it himself. These are the kinds of sermons that should make up the bulk of a pastor's preaching. "Although in many cases topical sermons are not only allowable, but very proper, those sermons which expound the exact words of the Holy Spirit are the most useful and the most agreeable to the major part of our congregations."[27]

Theological

His very first sermon as a nineteen-year-old guest preacher at the New Park Street Chapel was on James 1:17, on the "Father

---

[27] *Lectures* 1:75.

of lights, with whom is no variableness, neither shadow of turning" (KJV). The sermon, which he had recently preached at his
own church in Waterbeach was on divine immutability. Even as a
teenager, Spurgeon did not shy away from preaching doctrinally
weighty sermons. About a year later, on Sunday morning, January
7, 1855, Spurgeon preached another sermon on the same theme,
entitled, "The Immutability of God," from Malachi 3:6. This would
be the very first sermon published out of the sixty-three volumes of
sermons, perhaps a tribute to his first sermon at New Park Street.
Spurgeon opens in this way,

> It has been said by some one that "the proper study
> of mankind is man." I will not oppose the idea, but
> I believe it is equally true that the proper study of
> God's elect is God; the proper study of a Christian
> is the Godhead. The highest science, the lofti-
> est speculation, the mightiest philosophy, which
> can ever engage the attention of a child of God, is
> the name, the nature, the person, the work, the
> doings, and the existence of the great God whom
> he calls his Father. There is something exceed-
> ingly improving to the mind in a contemplation
> of the Divinity. It is a subject so vast, that all our
> thoughts are lost in its immensity; so deep, that
> our pride is drowned in its infinity.[28]

From the very beginning, Spurgeon committed to preaching
theologically rich sermons. He urged his students to follow his
example, "Brethren, if you are not theologians, you are in your pastorate just nothing at all. You may be fine rhetoricians . . . but without knowledge of the gospel, and the aptness to teach it, you are

---

[28] *NPSP* 1:1.

but a sounding brass and tinkling cymbal."[29] Gifted preachers often hid their theological ignorance behind their eloquence, humor, and charisma. These things were no substitute for sound doctrine and deep thought. Without theological sermons, churches starved for good food. Preachers were called to feed their people from the meat of the Word.

Spurgeon also believed in the importance of sound doctrine for protecting preachers from error. Even as he emphasized expositional preaching, Spurgeon saw many preachers attempt to preach difficult texts without a solid theological framework, leading them into error. "Many preachers are not theologians, and hence the mistakes which they make. It cannot do any hurt to the most lively evangelist to be also a sound theologian, and it may often be the means of saving him from gross blunders."[30] Scripture must interpret Scripture, and theology guards the preacher from error.

But more than just protecting the church, Spurgeon believed that theology revealed the riches of God's truth to the church. On one occasion, he envisioned the gospel "like a cavern into which you must enter bearing the torch of the Holy Spirit." As you first enter, you cry for joy at the precious metals that line the walls, but the Spirit takes you further into the cavern and each chamber is "more lofty and more spacious than the last. The floor, the roof, and the pendant stalactites [are] all of gold." Even as we marvel at the truth of Scripture and think there is no more to be seen, still "no mortal hath fully seen God's glory as yet, and the Divine Spirit waits to lead you by study and prayer to a yet clearer vision of the deep things of God."[31] The call of the pastor-theologian, then, is to explore the depths of the gospel and to bring the deep things of God for the joy of his people.

---

[29] *Lectures* 1:74.
[30] *AARM* 43–44.
[31] *AARM* 119.

Simple

But being a theological preacher was of no value to the people if a preacher did not know how to communicate God's Word effectively. Combined with his commitment to expositional preaching and sound theology was also a commitment to preaching with simplicity. Spurgeon once quipped, "The Lord Jesus did not say, 'Feed my giraffes,' but 'Feed my sheep.'"[32] Indeed, his congregation tended to be made up of the working class of London, or lower. Many had little to no education. Some were illiterate. Therefore, when preaching on themes like divine immutability, predestination, or the hypostatic union, he preached them in a way his people could understand.

This meant that Spurgeon could not rely on technical theological terms like the ones just mentioned. Of course, such terms were important to learn, but Spurgeon never assumed that his people understood them. Rather, he was careful to define, illustrate, and apply them. His goal was to speak plainly and not hide behind obscure terms.

> Be sure, moreover, to speak plainly; because, however excellent your matter, if a man does not comprehend it, it can be of no use to him; you might as well have spoken to him in the language of Kamskatka as in your own tongue, if you use phrases that are quite out of his line, and modes of expression which are not suitable to his mind.[33]

Of course, this kind of plainness is hard work. Spurgeon believed one must "go up to his level if [the listener] is a poor man;

---

[32] C. H. Spurgeon, *The Salt-Cellars: Being a Collection of Proverbs Together with Homely Notes Thereon*, Vols. 1–2, (London: Passmore & Alabaster, 1889-1891), 1:56.

[33] *Lectures* 1:141.

[and] go down to his understanding if he is an educated person." To speak to the uneducated, one must "walk in a path where your auditors can accompany you, and not to mount the high horse and ride over their heads."[34] Simplicity in preaching was especially emphasized in the Pastor's College. To cultivate this, Spurgeon urged them not to lose contact with the realities and challenges of life. Though traditional colleges tended to remove students from natural settings, Spurgeon's students lived with families, remained active in church, interacted with people from all walks of life, and actively ministered while they studied. All this was part of their education. The last thing Spurgeon wanted was to breed an artificiality in his students' preaching.[35]

In the end, simplicity in preaching was about gospel clarity. Rather than pursuing eloquence, the preacher should speak in whatever way was needed to get the gospel across. "Speak from your heart, and never mind about eloquence. Do not speak after the manner of the orator; speak as a lover of souls, and then you will have real eloquence."[36] Too often, the pursuit of unnatural preaching styles came from a desire for respectability, not a love for the listener. But a confidence in the truth of the gospel produces preachers who aim for simplicity.[37]

---

[34] *Lectures* 1:141.

[35] "We think it a fit thing that students who are to become ministers in sympathy with the people, should continue in association with ordinary humanity. To abstract them altogether from family life, and collect them under one roof, may have its advantages, but it has counterbalancing dangers. It is artificial, and is apt to breed artificialness. It may be objected, that residing, as our men do, with our friends around, they may be disturbed by the various family incidents. But why should they not? . . . Recluse life or collegiate life is not the life of the many, and much of it soon puts a man out of harmony with the everyday affairs of life." *S&T* 1871:227.

[36] *AARM* 129.

[37] "The preacher must also mind that he preaches Christ very simply. He must break up his big words and long sentences, and pray against the temptation to use

Evangelistic

The very first sermon that Spurgeon preached at the newly constructed Metropolitan Tabernacle on March 25, 1861, was on Acts 5:42, "And daily in the temple, and in every house, they ceased not to teach and preach Jesus Christ" (KJV). In this sermon, Spurgeon made a definitive statement about his preaching,

> I would propose that the subject of the ministry of this house, as long as this platform shall stand, and as long as this house shall be frequented by worshippers, shall be the person of Jesus Christ. I am never ashamed to avow myself a Calvinist. . . . I do not hesitate to take the name of Baptist . . . but if I am asked to say what is my creed, I think I must reply—"It is Jesus Christ." My venerable predecessor, Dr. Gill, has left a body of divinity, admirable and excellent in its way, but the body of divinity to which I would pin and bind myself for ever, God helping me, is not his system of divinity or any other human treatise, but Christ Jesus, who is the sum and substance of the gospel; who is in himself all theology the incarnation of every precious truth, the all-glorious personal embodiment of the way, the truth, and the life.[38]

Spurgeon carried this out throughout his preaching ministry. Wherever he was preaching, whether in the Mosaic law, or the prophets, or the epistles, Spurgeon always found his way to Christ

---

them. It is usually the short, dagger-like sentence that does the work best. . . . He must employ a simple, homely style, or such a style as God has given him; and he must preach Christ so plainly that his hearers can not only understand him, but that they cannot misunderstand him even if they try to do so." *MTP* 56:489.

[38] *MTP* 7:169.

from every part of Scripture. Just as every road in England eventually led to London, so Spurgeon believed that every text of Scripture (and thus, every sermon) should have a road to Christ. Other doctrines like perseverance or election were important but secondary. "Whatever we do not preach, let us preach Jesus Christ."[39]

Still, his commitment to preach Christ did not mean that he avoided preaching the imperatives of the Christian life. Depending on his text, he would preach both the grace of the gospel and the demands of the law. He addressed both individual sins and societal sins. He challenged Christians outside and inside his denomination. When speaking to his congregation, he thought about different categories among his people and applied God's Word to each group specifically. "Consider the condition of your hearers. Reflect upon their spiritual state as a whole and as individuals, and prescribe the medicine adapted to the current disease, or prepare the food suitable for the prevailing necessity."[40]

Regardless of his audience, their spiritual condition, or the challenges of their context, Spurgeon believed that their primary need was to hear the gospel. Only through repentance and faith in Christ could sinners be saved. But in using the term *gospel*, he did not reduce his message to an abstract plan of salvation or a theoretical idea. No, for Spurgeon, preaching the gospel meant preaching Christ, in all his glory. "Of all I would wish to say this is the sum; my brethren, preach CHRIST, always and evermore. He is the whole gospel. His person, offices, and work must be our one great, all-comprehending theme. The world needs still to be told of its Savior, and of the way to reach him."[41]

The preaching of Christ should not, however, be limited to individual salvation. Spurgeon believed that Christ was the solution to

---

[39] *MTP* 19:381.
[40] *Lectures* 1:90.
[41] *Lectures* 1:82.

all societal ills. In his sermon, "How to Meet the Evils of the Age," Spurgeon walks through a litany of discouraging contemporary challenges that Christians faced in his day both in the church and in society. But then he offers the remedy,

> I have only one remedy to prescribe, and that is, that we do preach the gospel of our Lord and Savior, Jesus Christ, in all its length and breadth of doctrine, precept, spirit, example, and power. . . . We have only to preach the living gospel, and the whole of it, to meet the whole of the evils of the times. The gospel, if it were fully received through the whole earth, would purge away all slavery and all war, and put down all drunkenness and all social evils; in fact, you cannot conceive a moral curse which it would not remove; and even physical evils, since many of them arise incidentally from sin, would be greatly mitigated, and some of them for ever abolished.[42]

Committed to preaching Christ, Spurgeon was convinced the world needed no other remedy. As sinful hearts were redeemed and transformed, as people lived out their faith in their communities, workplaces, and nations, Spurgeon believed the gospel could truly impact the world.

Dependent

Finally, and most importantly, Spurgeon believed in his absolute dependence on the Holy Spirit in his preaching. "To us, as ministers, the Holy Spirit is absolutely essential. Without him our office is a mere name."[43] This has been evident in the preceding points. In

---

[42] *AARM* 112–113.
[43] *Lectures* 2:3.

preparing his sermon, Spurgeon relied on the Spirit when select-
ing a text and to illuminate the text for him. Prior to each service,
Spurgeon spent time in prayer with his deacons and elders, "dependent upon the Lord for every particle of strength."[44] In preaching a
sermon, Spurgeon did not rely on a manuscript. He depended on
the Spirit "to open our mouths that we may show forth the praises
of the Lord" and "to keep us back from saying many things which, if
they actually left our tongue, would mar our message."[45]

Spurgeon's reliance on the Spirit was not merely for his own
performance but for the salvation of souls. Preaching is the work of
man, but salvation is the work of God. Spurgeon preached knowing
that as much as he had prepared and worked at his preaching, he
was still utterly helpless to bring about the conversion of a soul. He
looked to God alone for such results.[46]

Spurgeon also rejoiced that salvation did not depend on his
feeble efforts. If salvation belonged to the Lord, then God could use
a sermon to save 1,000 sinners as much as He could save one. The
power lay not in the preacher but in God's omnipotence. Spurgeon's
dependence on the Spirit was combined with a strong faith that God
would fulfill His promise to work powerfully through His Word.
And so, he preached with boldness.

---

[44] *MTP* 36:400.

[45] *MTP* 36:400.

[46] "Look you, sir, you may study your sermon; you may examine the original
of your text; you may critically follow it out in all its bearings; you may go and
preach it with great correctness of expression; but you cannot quicken a soul by
that sermon. You may go up into your pulpit. You may illustrate, explain, and
enforce the truth. With mighty rhetoric, you may charm your hearers—you may
hold them spellbound—but no eloquence of yours can raise the dead. . . . Another
voice than ours must be heard; other power than that of thought or persuasion
must be brought into the work, or it will not be done. . . . Only as the Spirit
of God shall bless men by you, shall they receive a blessing through you." *MTP*
38:111–112.

The Prayer and Hope of Preaching: Revival

The aim of preaching is faithfulness. The preacher's task is to preach God's Word accurately and faithfully, and then to leave the results to God. However, a preacher is never content to only preach faithful sermons regardless of the results. Rather, his prayer is that sinners would be converted, and the church be built up. Even more, his prayer is for revival.

Spurgeon believed that in certain seasons of the church's history, the Holy Spirit moved in the church in powerful ways. Under the preaching of the English Puritans in the seventeenth century and Whitefield and Wesley in the eighteenth century, England experienced times of revival when the church was awakened to the glory of Christ and sinners were converted in large numbers. Yet as remarkable as previous revivals might be, the church cannot live in the past. Every generation needs the surprising work of God in their day.

But what does revival look like? In 1858, Spurgeon preached a sermon entitled, "The Great Revival," where he reflected on the phenomenon of revival. The preacher suddenly finds the chapel filled with visitors coming to hear the preaching of God's Word. "There are the people, and how they listen! They are all awake, all in earnest; they lean their heads forward, they put their hands to their ears; his voice is feeble, they try to help him; they are doing anything so that they may hear the Word of Life." As a result, the church begins to pray. Prayer-meetings that were once scarcely attended are now filled with "five or six hundred. . . . And oh! how they pray!"

The members of the church now give attention to their own private lives. Family worship is restored. Parents bring their children to Sunday school and earnestly pray for their conversion. Their conversation is no longer marked by gossip or idle talk. Instead, they speak of the things of God and seek to edify one another.

Then comes the grand result:

> There is an inquirers' meeting held; the good
> brother who presides over it is astonished, he never
> saw so many coming in his life before. "Why," says
> he, "there is a hundred, at least, come to confess
> what the Lord has done for their souls! Here are
> fifty come all at once to say that under such a ser-
> mon they were brought to the knowledge of the
> truth. Who hath begotten me these? How hath it
> come about? How can it be? Is not the Lord a great
> God that hath wrought such a work as this?"[47]

Infused with the joy and life of these new converts, the church
is transformed. Their singing is "like the crashing thunder." Their
prayers are "like the swift, sharp dash of lightning, lighting up the
darkness of the cold hearted, and making them for a moment feel
that there is something in prayer." And their gatherings are marked
by "hearty good-will." Everything is done with an eye to God's glory.

Such revival can even touch wider society as a city, region, and
nation is moved by the preaching of the Word. And the results of
revival extend into eternity, as heaven is filled with the songs of
the saints and the joy of the angels. "The universe is made glad;
it is God's own summer; it is the universal spring. The time of the
singing of birds is come; the voice of the turtle is heard in our
land. Oh! that God might send us such a revival of religion as this!"
Spurgeon's description of revival mirrors his own experience, seeing the churches in Waterbeach and London transformed by the
preaching of God's Word.

But the million-dollar question is: How does it all begin? How
does revival come upon the church? The answer is that it all begins

---

[47] *NPSP* 4:164–65.

with the preacher. Just as snow, melted by the sun, runs down
the mountain and waters the valleys, so the preacher, revived by
the Spirit, blesses the church.[48] And so, even as he prepares and
preaches faithful sermons, his prayer is first and foremost for himself, that God would do a work in his life, so that the church might
be blessed under the preaching of the Word.

Conclusion

Most pastors today are busy. They juggle all kinds of responsibilities: overseeing ministries, managing staff, attending meetings,
visiting the sick, caring for the facilities, planning budgets, counsel-
ing the hurting, organizing committees, and the list goes on and
on. Amid the busy-ness, it is difficult to prioritize responsibilities.

As a busy pastor himself, Spurgeon provides guidance. The primary calling of a pastor is to preach God's Word faithfully. With
all the pastoral responsibilities that Spurgeon took on, he never
compromised his ability to feed his congregation richly from God's
Word week after week. As his responsibilities grew, Spurgeon
recruited the help he needed to ensure that the preaching of the
Word did not suffer. If you are church member or lay leader in the
church, how can you pray for your pastor in his preaching? How
can you take responsibilities off his plate so that he can give himself
more fully to that work?

As a busy pastor, the most loving thing you can do for your
people is to give yourself to preaching faithful, Christ-exalting sermons week after week. That's not to say you should lock yourself in

---

[48] "The revival has touched the minister; the sun, shining so brightly, has
melted some of the snow on the mountain-top, and it is running down in fertil-
izing streams, to bless the valleys; and the people down below are refreshed by
the ministrations of the man of God who has awakened himself up from his sleep,
and finds himself, like another Elijah, made strong for forty days of labor." *NPSP*
4:164–65.

your study throughout the week. As we'll see in subsequent chapters, pastoral ministry involves more than preaching. But it is not less than preaching. It must involve giving ourselves to the work of proclaiming God's Word to God's people. And as we do so, we pray with hope that God will use His Word to revive His church.

THE VERY GATE OF HEAVEN
CHURCH GATHERINGS

Rooted in the Church

Charles Spurgeon grew up in the church. At ten months old, his parents needed some help, so he was sent to live with his grandparents. Spurgeon's grandfather, James, was the Congregationalist minister in the town of Stambourne. Many of Spurgeon's earliest memories deal with the meetings of the church. He recalls the peg behind the pulpit where his grandfather hung his hat, the elders sitting solemnly beneath the pulpit, the square pews with curtains, and the sounding board over the pulpit, which made the preacher look like a Jack-in-the-box. Like many bored children, Spurgeon entertained himself during long sermons with the various details of the room.

By age six, Spurgeon moved back to live with his parents in Colchester. His experience with the church there was not nearly as positive as his time in Stambourne. Still, the church continued to play a prominent role in his life. At times, Spurgeon and his siblings played church, and of course, he was the preacher. He also formed the "Home Juvenile Society" for the neighborhood kids, complete with a handwritten magazine, business meetings, and prayer meetings. When off to school in Maidstone and Newmarket, he continued to attend local church services each week, even though he knew he was unconverted. At Newmarket, he befriended a cook at the school who loved discussing theology. They both attended the same church and disliked the preaching. Spurgeon once asked her why she even bothered going. She responded, "I like to go out to worship even if I get nothing by going. You see a hen sometimes scratching all over a heap of rubbish to try to find some corn; she does not get any, but it shows that she is looking for it, and using the means to get it, and then, too, the exercise warms her."[1] At a young age, Spurgeon was being discipled in a commitment to the gatherings of the church. But as much as he religiously attended church, it did not ease the guilt of his conscience.[2]

Salvation was not found in the outward participation of corporate worship. Rather, it was through the preaching of the Word that Spurgeon came to believe the gospel. On a wintry Lord's Day gathering of a Primitive Methodist congregation, Spurgeon heard the gospel and was converted. That evening he attended the Baptist chapel in Colchester and was encouraged in his newfound faith.

We can continue to trace this theme of corporate worship throughout Spurgeon's young Christian life: faithfully attending the Congregational church in Newmarket, being baptized at a baptismal service of the Baptist congregation in Isleham, and eventually worshiping at St. Andrew's Street in Cambridge while working as a tutor. It was through the lay preaching association at St. Andrew's that Spurgeon would have his first preaching opportunities and eventually be called as the pastor of Waterbeach Chapel in the fall of

---

[1] *Autobiography* 1:53.

[2] "I used to feel myself to be a sinner even when I was in the house of God. I thought that, when I sang, I was mocking the Lord with a solemn sound upon a false tongue; and if I prayed, I feared that I was sinning in my prayers, insulting Him by uttering confessions which I did not feel, and asking for mercies with a faith that was not true at all, but only another form of unbelief." *Autobiography* 1:82.

1851. For the rest of his life, his work would involve organizing and leading the corporate worship of congregations.

This chapter will explore Spurgeon's leadership of the corporate worship at the Metropolitan Tabernacle. As the pastor, he took responsibility not only for the preaching but also for every aspect of the corporate gatherings, from the hymns to the prayers, to the Scripture readings. What's remarkable is that for thirty-eight years of pastoral ministry, his services varied very little. And yet, thousands kept returning week after week to be edified by that worship. My prayer is that there would be something for us to learn from Spurgeon's example. We will examine first his convictions about the corporate gatherings of the church, then we will consider how he practically carried them out.

Not Forsaking the Assembling of Ourselves Together

For the Christian, the worship of God overflows into every aspect of life. Spurgeon believed singing, prayer, and Scripture reading should not be limited to the gatherings of the church but should take place both in public and in private: "Public worship is not everything; if there were no private worship, it would be nothing by itself. . . . The man who does not meet God outside the temple will not meet God inside the temple, he may rest assured of that."[3] Private worship proved the genuineness of public worship.

At the same time, Spurgeon believed that public worship was a necessity. It was commanded by God. It was not enough to only worship in private. As in our day, there was no shortage of excuses for people in the nineteenth century to forsake assembling together. With the growth of printed sermons, many Christians found it

---

[3] *MTP* 41:14.

easier to pick the latest sermon from their favorite preachers and stay home. But commenting on Hebrews 10:25, Spurgeon declared,

> There are some who even make a bad use of what ought to be a great blessing, namely, the printing-press, and the printed sermon, by staying at home to read a sermon because, they say, it is better than going out to hear one. Well, dear friend, if I could not hear profitably, I would still make one of the assembly gathered together for the worship of God. It is a bad example for a professing Christian to absent himself from the assembly of the friends of Christ. There was a dear sister, whom many of you knew, who used to attend here with great regularity, although she could not hear a word that was said; but she said it did her good to join in the hymns, and to know that she was worshipping God with the rest of his people. I wish that some, who stay away for the most frivolous excuses, would think of this verse: "Not forsaking the assembling of ourselves together, as the manner of some is."[4]

In other words, the gatherings of the church were for more than just individual edification (which might be gained through a printed sermon). They were about "worshipping God with the rest of his people" and being a part of "the assembly of the friends of Christ." In gathering with the church, we demonstrate that we belong to God's people.

At the same time, Spurgeon also believed that the gatherings of the church were a means of grace in the Christian life. As the saints gathered to sing psalms, hymns, and spiritual songs, offer their

---

[4] *MTP* 48:610.

prayers together, and hear the reading and preaching of the Word, God used these activities to strengthen their faith in Christ and love for one another. While such activity could never earn God's grace, every Christian should still attend the gatherings of the church with an expectation of God's blessing. "God may bless us when we are not in his house, but we have the best reason to hope that he will when we are in communion with his saints."[5]

We should, however, not imagine God's grace as impersonal. Rather, Spurgeon saw God's grace given personally through Christ's presence with the church. Even as Christ promised to be with His people individually, He also promised to be with them as they are gathered in His name. Christ "delights most of all to come into the assembly of his servants."[6]

Therefore, Spurgeon would not dare miss out on the gatherings of the church . . . not because he feared missing out on some blessing or breaking some rule; it was because he did not want to miss out on the joy of communing with Christ and His people! The gathering of the church is the closest the Christian gets to heaven on this side of eternity.

> To forsake the assembling of ourselves together would involve the loss of one of the dearest Christian privileges, for the worship of the church below is the vestibule of the adoration of heaven. If ever heaven comes down to earth it is in the communion of saints. Our Lord's table is oftentimes

---

[5] *MTP* 9:688.

[6] "Though our Lord may reveal himself to single individuals in solitude . . . yet he more usually shows himself to two or three, and he delights most of all to come into the assembly of his servants. The Lord seems most at home when, standing in the midst of his people, he says, 'Peace be unto you.' Let us not fail to meet with our fellow believers. For my part, the assemblies of God's people shall ever be dear to me. . . . Oh, that we may behold the Lord Jesus in the present assembly!" *MTP* 30:205.

glory anticipated. The prayer meeting often seems to be held close to Jerusalem's city wall; it stands in a sort of border land between the celestial and the terrestrial; it is a house and yet a gate, fruition and expectation in one, the house of God and the very gate of heaven.[7]

Many visitors who attended the gatherings at the Metropolitan Tabernacle testified to their sense of heavenly realities as they worshiped with the congregation. In the hearing of God's Word, in the singing of God's praises, in the offering of prayers, these Sabbath gatherings were a time of great joy in Christ.

Christ Alone Is the Lawmaker of the Church

In connecting the gathering of the church to heaven, Spurgeon taught his people that their worship services were an expression of Christ's reign on earth. Therefore, the church's gatherings must be ruled by the Word of Christ. Conversely, human preferences or traditions had no final authority in the church. Spurgeon never used the term, but this is what the Reformers before him called the Regulative Principle. He explains it like this:

> Christ alone is the lawmaker of the church and no rule or regulation in the Christian church standeth for anything unless in its spirit at least it hath the mind of Christ to support and back it up. . . . When we meet together in church meeting we cannot make laws for the Lord's kingdom; we dare not attempt it. Such necessary regulations as may be made for carrying out our Lord's commands,

---

[7] S&T 1868:339–40.

to meet for worship, and to proclaim the gospel, are commendable, because they are acts needful to obedience to his highest laws; but even these minor details are not tolerable if they clearly violate the spirit and mind of Jesus Christ. He has rather given us spiritual guidances than legal rubrics and fettering liturgies, and he has left us at liberty to follow the directions of his own free Spirit.[8]

The Regulative Principle taught that Christ alone is the lawmaker of the church and everything should be ordered according to His Word. This is not to say that Christ's instructions for His church are all equally clear. In the areas of the church's activity and mission that are less clear from Scripture, rather than turning to "legal rubrics and fettering liturgies," the church should depend on the wisdom and guidance of the Spirit. Yet, as His assembled people, Christ reigns over His church and the church follows Christ's will in its worship and in all other matters.

For Spurgeon, this principle applied especially to the corporate worship of the church. In opposition to those who were drawn to a high liturgy stuffed with rituals and ceremonies, Spurgeon called his people to a simple adherence to God's Word. He saw explicit warrant for this in the Old Testament, as Israel was given very specific instructions by Moses for how they were to worship and approach God. In the same way, New Testament saints are to hold fast to the word of Christ as they gather for worship.[9]

---

[8] *MTP* 14:617–18.

[9] "When the tabernacle was pitched in the wilderness, what was the authority for its length and breadth? Why was the altar of incense to be placed here, and the brazen layer there? Why so many lambs or bullocks to be offered on a certain day? Why must the passover be roasted whole and not sodden? Simply and only because God had shown all these things to Moses in the holy mount; and thus had Jehovah spoken, 'Look that thou make them after their pattern, which was

A Simple Liturgy

The practical result of this conviction was the worship at the Metropolitan Tabernacle would be very simple. Churches in those days were experimenting with all kinds of new inventions in their worship services—different types of choirs, organs, entertainments, and more. But one of the hallmarks of the Tabernacle was that its worship remained largely the same as the days of its founding. As one deacon stated, "the services of religion have been conducted without any peculiarity of innovation. No musical or aesthetic accompaniments have ever been used. The weapons of our warfare are not carnal, but they are mighty."[10] The simplicity and consistency of their services reflected the conviction that the worship of God's people should only contain the elements commanded in God's Word.

The liturgy at the Tabernacle always consisted of three elements: prayer, congregational singing, and the ministry of the Word. These elements could be found in any worship gathering of the church, whether on Sunday morning or Thursday evening. A typical service included an opening prayer, the singing of hymns, the pastoral prayer, Scripture reading and exposition, the sermon, and a benediction. The ordinances of baptism and the Lord's Supper were also regularly observed, though not at every gathering.

Some Baptist churches held to the regulative principle so rigidly that they bristled at any change to their meeting space or order of service. Spurgeon warned his people, "You know it is quite as easy for a man to trust in ceremonials, when they are severely simple, as for a man to rely upon them when they are gorgeous and superb. A man may as much trust in the simple ordinance of immersion and

---

showed thee in the mount.' It is even so in the Church at the present day; true servants of God demand to see for all Church ordinances and doctrines the express authority of the Church's only Teacher and Lord." *MTP* 10:591.

    10 *NPSP* 5:350.

the breaking of bread, as another may trust in the high mass and in the prayers of priests."[11] So as the one who planned all the services of the church, even as he held to the regulative principle, Spurgeon varied aspects of the service as he felt led. Speaking to his students, he advised them, "vary the order of service as much as possible. Whatever the free Spirit moves us to do, that let us do at once."[12] While the elements of Spurgeon's liturgy were fixed, he often varied the order of elements, the content of prayers, the number of hymns, the length of Scripture expositions, and more. Spurgeon once even commended a pastor for preaching the sermon at the beginning of the service, so that latecomers would be able to participate in the prayers and singing![13] All this not only guarded the congregation from becoming legalistic in their liturgy, but it helped them to engage thoughtfully in the worship by keeping things fresh.

The Weekly Rhythm

Every week, the congregation at the Metropolitan Tabernacle gathered four times for worship: Sunday morning, Sunday night, Monday night for prayer-meeting, and Thursday night. These were not multiple services as churches have them today. Each service was distinct, and Spurgeon expected his members to attend these services regularly.

Sunday Services

Unsurprisingly, the best attended services were the Sunday morning and evening services. Church members made up a large part of the congregation, especially as the church continued to grow. Visitors to London from other parts of the English-speaking

---

[11] *NPSP* 4:173–74.
[12] *Lectures* 1:68.
[13] *Lectures* 1:68.

world were also frequently in attendance. For many tourists, worshiping at the Metropolitan Tabernacle was at the top of their to-do lists. Sunday morning congregations were typically made up of the upper and middle classes. On Sunday evenings, though, the working and lower classes would join in the mix after work.

Londoners in the nineteenth century loved making the rounds and checking out the latest preacher. As a result, crowds were a constant challenge. Especially in the early years, Spurgeon struggled with seating and often had to turn people away. He often chided visiting members of other churches for taking up seats and neglecting their own churches. Because of the crowds, Spurgeon issued tickets for his services. Members and supporters of the ministry could reserve tickets with an assigned pew that allowed them to enter the building early through a side entrance. After early admission, five minutes prior to the service, the front doors would open, and the general population could enter the building and occupy any spare seats. The pews also had flaps that could be lowered to provide seating along the aisles and people sometimes also stood along walls. Once the service started, any unoccupied reserved seat was made available.

Because the demand for tickets was so great, not every member could get a ticket. Some of the newer members who were unfamiliar with the ticketing system had to wait for general admission. But in their eagerness to worship with God's people, they were happy to wait. Spurgeon recounts,

> Many have been the young Christians who have joined this church, and old ones too and I have said to them, "Well, have you got a ticket for a seat?"
>
> "No, sir." "Well, what will you do? Have you got a preference ticket?"

"No, I cannot get one, but I do not mind standing in the crowd an hour, or two hours. I will come
at five o'clock so that I can get in. Sometimes I
don't get in, sir; but even then I feel that I have
done what I ought to do in attempting to get in."
"Well," but I have said, "you live five miles off, and
there is coming and going back twice a day—you
cannot do it." "Oh, sir," they have said "I can do
it; I feel so much the blessedness of the Sabbath
and so much enjoyment of the presence of the
Savior."[14]

Because of the demand for admission tickets, members of the
church sometimes used them as evangelistic tools, giving them to
their neighbors for a Sunday service and urging them to attend,
while they stood in the back.

What was a typical Sunday service at the Metropolitan
Tabernacle like? We have many eyewitness accounts of these ser-
vices. Not every visitor enjoyed their time. Writing in his diary,
Samuel Clemens (Mark Twain) records his experience in 1879:

Sunday, August 17, '79. Raw and cold, and a
drenching rain. Went to hear Mr. Spurgeon. House
three-quarters full—say three thousand people.
First hour, lacking one minute, taken up with two
prayers, two ugly hymns, and Scripture-reading.
Sermon three-quarters of an hour long. A fluent
talker, good, sonorous voice. Topic treated in the
unpleasant, old fashion: Man a mighty bad child,
God working at him in forty ways and having a
world of trouble with him.

---

[14] *NPSP* 4:419.

> A wooden-faced congregation; just the sort to
> see no incongruity in the majesty of Heaven stoop-
> ing to plead and sentimentalize over such, and see
> in their salvation an important matter.[15]

What I appreciate about this account is that Spurgeon never felt any need to alter the content of his services or the preaching to entertain visitors.[16] While the preaching may have been impressive in an oratorical sense, those with no appreciation of spiritual truth likely walked away from the service unimpressed, even bored. This was intentional on Spurgeon's part. These services were aimed at regenerate believers and for calling sinners to salvation in Christ.

For true Christians who attended the services at the Tabernacle with a sense of holy expectation, their experience was very different. The service itself often left a greater impression than the preaching. Beyond walking through the elements of the service, it would be hard to convey what it would have been like to attend a service at the Metropolitan Tabernacle during Spurgeon's ministry. Perhaps our best glimpse is through the eyewitness accounts that remain. Justin Fulton, a pastor from Boston visiting in 1868 shares his experience:

> The first prayer was short and general in charac-
> ter, but very devout. No fooling here, we are met

---

[15] Albert Bigelow Paine, *Mark Twain, a Biography: The Personal and Literary Life of Samuel Langhorne Clemens* (United Kingdom: Harper & Brothers, 1912), 647. It appears from his diary that Clemens had a better time the following Tuesday visiting Windermere Lake and talking with "the great Darwin."

[16] The sermon preached by Spurgeon during Clemens's visit is titled "Contention Ended and Grace Reigning," *MTP* 25:469–80. The songs sung from Spurgeon's *Our Own Hymn-Book: A Collection of Psalms and Hymns for Public, Social, and Private Worship* (London: Passmore & Alabaster, 1885), hymn 194, 591, and 586; "Up to the Lord that Reigns on High" by Isaac Watts; "Saviour, When in Dust to Thee" by Robert Grant; and "Approach My Soul, the Mercy Seat" by John Newton.

to worship God. The first hymn was sung with a will. No chanting or piping organ, no choir to attract attention, but one grand purpose to glorify our Christ. We sang out of "Our Own Hymn Book." Everything has Mr. Spurgeon's imprint. If you don't like it you can leave it; here is a concern big enough to run without your help. Fall into the current or be swept away. I fell in with my whole heart, as happy as a seraph.

Then came the reading of the Scriptures. Time enough. No hurry. How those English people did enjoy the word of God! The second prayer followed. That was my prayer, because it was everybody's cry. His prayer was greater to me than his sermon. In his sermon he talked with men. In his prayer he communed with God. When he described the coming of Christ to the soul, it seemed to me I saw for the first time The King in His beauty. The suppliant was forgiven. With his face streaming with tears, and with tones so full and rich that they swept through every heart, as a breath of perfumed air floats through the halls of a palace, this divine atmosphere possessed our hearts when he cried: "We love thee. Thou knowest it. We love not because thou art great, but because of the inestimable gift of thy only begotten Son. Lift us up O God. Take us out of the dust. Let us by faith come to the fountain and be washed. We come. We feel that thou hast washed us. We are clean. Yes, we are clean. Blessed be the Lord our God. Make us young again. Wake us up. Let us not sleep. We thank thee for our troubles, for all that makes us conscious of our alienation from thee. Bless our Orphanage, our College, our Retreat," and so on he went, enumerating every claim, and presenting the requests so naturally that every heart joined in the up going petition. The close of the prayer lingers as a memory which does not die.

"We close our prayer as to the words. We have been with thee. We know it. Thou hast heard us and blessed us. We feel it. We retire from the mercy-seat thanking thee for audience and praying for thy blessing on us all."

Another hymn better than the first, because now all were in a worshiping mood, was sung. In the singing he was an inspiration. His happy look, his determined air, his wonderful voice rang out sweeter and grander than any organ-peal I ever listened to at home or abroad.

His step was light and free. His gestures were graceful and telling. His text was found in Psalm 42:1 "As the hart panteth after the water brooks so panteth my soul after thee, O God." I was suited to the highest and best form of dramatic art. I can see him now, as without a pulpit or a note he stood before 6,000 people, every eye on him, picturing that hart on the mountain's brow, thirsty, ears back, tongue out, hunted and almost famishing from thirst, seeing the brook running through the valley in the distance, and then without a care making for it by leaping from crag to crag until he reaches the stream there to slake his burning thirst. The entire audience drank with the hart, and were refreshed. After this in love he portrayed the Christian's thirst. How dry we became. Then he uncovered the fountain in Christ. It seemed to me that I had never seen my Christ before. There he was in his beauty. That morning all saw him and were refreshed. It was good to be there.[17]

Monday Night Prayer Meeting

In addition to the prayers offered in the worship service, the congregation regularly met on Monday evenings for a congregational prayer meeting. It is impossible to overstate how important prayer was in Spurgeon's view of the health and ministry of church.

The prayer-meeting is not a farce, no waste of time, no mere pious amusement. Some in these times think so, but such shall be lightly esteemed. Surely they know not the omnipotence that lies in the pleas of God's people. The Lord has taken the keys of his royal treasury, and put them into the hand of faith. He has taken his sword from the scabbard, and given it into the hand of the man mighty in prayer. He seems at times to have placed his sovereign scepter in the hand of prayer.[18]

Do not let us become poor in prayer. It is a bad thing to become poor in money, because we need it for a thousand causes, and cannot get on without it. But we can do without money better than we can do without prayer. We must have your prayers.[19]

---

[17] Justin D. Fulton, *Spurgeon, Our Ally* (Brooklyn, NY: The Pauline Propaganda, 1923), 220–23.

[18] *MTP* 30:38–39.

[19] *MTP* 14:35.

> To strengthen a prayer-meeting is as good a work
> as to preach a sermon. I would have you vow that
> the prayer-meeting shall never be given up while
> you live.[20]

Spurgeon believed that God's saving work would not happen apart from the prayers of His people. Preaching was only half of the work. The congregation must support that work by constant, ardent prayer. If you complained to Spurgeon about your pastor's preaching, he would likely respond by asking you, "Well, are you praying for him and for the ministry of the Word?" Spurgeon believed in the importance of church structures and polity, but he did not see the church simply as an engine to keep running mechanically. Instead, the church is a living organism, motivated by spiritual life and dependence on God. And that dependence must be expressed in prayer.[21]

Therefore, after the Sunday services, the most important gathering of the church was the church prayer meeting, held on Monday nights in the main auditorium. While dozens of smaller prayer meetings were held throughout the week in homes and before the services, this was the weekly meeting where the whole church came together to pray. More than a thousand members regularly attended, along with visitors and other Christian workers. After a hymn and Scripture reading with commentary, the chair (often Spurgeon, sometimes a deacon or an elder) read through requests for prayer or called on someone to share about particular requests. As requests were shared, various church officers and members of

---

[20] S&T 1881:494.

[21] "It seems to me that the most Scriptural system of Church government is that which requires the most prayer, the most faith, and the most piety, to keep it going. The Church of God was never meant to be an automaton. . . . The Church was meant to be a living thing, a living person, and as the person cannot be supported, if life be absent, or if food be kept back, or if breath be suspended, so should it be with the Church." MTP 7:366.

the church, including Spurgeon, led in prayer for those items. The congregation participated in the prayers, voicing their Amens. After a lengthy time of sharing and prayer, a brief address was given (often by Spurgeon) and before long, it was 8:30 p.m. and the meeting was concluded.

Spurgeon believed that prayer meetings should not become monotonous or formal. To help maintain freshness, he varied the theme of prayer meetings from time to time. By default, prayer-meetings were devoted to praying for the members of the church and their ministries. This included praying for healing, but these were often connected with some spiritual theme. Many prayers were for lost loved ones and for fruit in their evangelistic efforts. These meetings would sometimes include a baptismal service and prayer for new members.

Other meetings were devoted to the ministries of the church. Whenever a significant institution, like the Orphanage or the Colportage Association or the Sunday School Union, might have their annual meeting on a Monday afternoon, the Monday night prayer-meeting would be devoted to praying for their ministry. New church plants were also commissioned at the prayer meeting and the night was devoted to praying for the new work.

Prayer meetings were sometimes organized by theme. For example, in one meeting, Spurgeon shared "that *the cross* was to furnish the key-note for the whole meeting. Prayers would be offered for a revival of the pure doctrine of the cross, for the exhibition of the pure life of cross-bearing, and for a revival of that earnestness and consecration which are the true outgrowth of the cross of Christ."[22] Once a month, the meeting was devoted entirely to praying for missions. At those meetings, well-known figures like Hudson Taylor, Johann Oncken, or one of their associates might

---

[22] *S&T* 1881:630.

be present to share about their work abroad. Often, updates from missionaries and Pastors' College graduates were shared either via a letter or in person. In later years, Spurgeon was especially glad to include his sons Charles and Thomas among those for whom the congregation prayed.

But the Metropolitan Tabernacle's prayer meeting was remarkable not only for its size and consistency, but also for its influence. Visitors from all over the world "carried away with them even to distant lands influences and impulses which they never wished to lose or to forget."[23] In an effort to promote prayer-meetings in other churches, Spurgeon published several accounts in *The Sword and the Trowel* of the ones that took place at the Tabernacle. His students also learned the importance of prayer. Whenever they wrote back to report on the progress of their churches, the main indicator of health was that their prayer meetings were well-attended. These reports reflected Spurgeon's conviction that "these meetings are the furnace by which the church-engine is supplied with power."[24]

To provide an eyewitness account of a prayer-meeting, let's turn to Fulton once again. This account shares his experience of a prayer meeting in 1868 at the Tabernacle. A large crowd was present as usual. But strangely, the meeting that week seemed dead. "All sang old tunes in an old-fashioned way. Nothing yet to explain the marvelous crowd. The Scripture was read, and the comment on it was good, but nothing surprising. . . . The prayers were in no way extraordinary." Then Deacon Olney got up and read through the requests for prayer and led the congregation in prayer, but "the meeting was still dead." Spurgeon then introduced his father who was also a minister and who spoke a few words. But the meeting dragged on. Every church will struggle with prayer meetings that feel dry and lifeless. The Tabernacle was no different.

---

[23] *Autobiography* 4:81.
[24] *S&T* 1881:91.

At that point, Olney said to Spurgeon, "You had better take the meeting." After a moment of silent preparation, Spurgeon rose to pray, and Fulton records the prayer in his account:

> "Oh God! Here is the Devil doing his best to break up this prayer-meeting. I hear him saying 'Spurgeon's prayer-meeting is a failure. The Church is dead,' he says. 'Faith,' he claims, 'is dying out.' I hear him, Lord, claiming that the people are satisfied with the collections, and the great congregations, and that they are letting go of the right hand of the Lord Jesus, in whom is all the might and power, now and forever more.
>
> "It is a lie, O God. There is not a bit of truth in what the Devil claims. We trust in thee, Jesus." Then he praised his Christ. He warmed to the theme. Then the Amens began to roll forth.
>
> "Come, Jesus, lift us out of ourselves and into thee."
>
> "Amen!" was our united shout; it was done.[25]

Certainly, not every prayer-meeting was that dramatic. The accounts of the prayer-meetings at the Tabernacle generally give a sense of the people walking away edified and encouraged by the ordinary work of praying and depending on their Lord. But perhaps that was the secret to Spurgeon's prayer meeting. These gatherings were crucial reminders to hold fast to Christ. Amid all their success and growth and activity, it would be too easy for a church to begin letting go of Christ's hand and trusting in their efforts and methods. The weekly prayer meeting helped ensure that activism and success never displaced their love for and dependence on Christ.

---

[25] Fulton, *Spurgeon, Our Ally*, 227–28.

Thursday Night Service

The last worship gathering of the week would be on Thursday nights. Beginning at 7:00 p.m., this mid-week service aimed to encourage his people in Christ amid the toils and pressures of life. Once again, the liturgy was simple: singing, prayer, and preaching. Sermons tended to be more extemporaneous, as Spurgeon would carry into the pulpit a simple outline and preach from the overflow of his heart.

One of the unique features of Thursday night services is that Christian workers from all denominations, who normally wouldn't be able to attend a Sunday service, could attend on Thursday nights. There were often many clergymen from the Church of England and ministers from Nonconformist churches present. In this way, Spurgeon's ministry extended to other churches in London as he refreshed their pastors during the week through the preaching of the Word. Many of them would stay after the service to speak with Spurgeon "so that it was late before he could get away."[26]

Thursday night services were also an opportunity for the non-churchgoing community to come hear Spurgeon, especially as the building was less crowded with visitors on those evenings. On one occasion the Bible Flower Mission of the church distributed the following invitation around the neighborhood:

> While people from all parts of the world crowd the Tabernacle every Sunday, we are sure that there are very many living almost under the shadow of the building who have never heard Mr. Spurgeon preach. He is going to the South of France in November, so we ask you to come and hear him on Thursday Evening during this month. The Service commences at 7 o'clock.[27]

---

[26] *Autobiography* 4:88.
[27] Bible Flower Mission Invitation, 1886, Metropolitan Tabernacle Archives, London.

In the weekly rhythm of the church, all four services played an important role in building up the congregation and reaching the community with the gospel.

The Pastor as Service Leader

As the pastor, Spurgeon believed he was not only responsible for preaching, but also for planning the worship gatherings of the church. This meant picking out the hymns, Scripture readings, preparing the prayers, and arranging the order of service. The simple liturgy combined with his vast knowledge of Scripture and hymnody made planning much easier. For the thousands of sermons that Spurgeon preached at the Metropolitan Tabernacle, he also planned the services to go along with them. We've already discussed Spurgeon's preaching, but now we should look at his approach to praying, Scripture readings, and singing.

Public Prayers

The worship service usually consisted of two prayers: the opening prayer and the pastoral prayer. The opening prayer reminded the congregation that they had come to worship God. There was often a loud buzz throughout the auditorium as the large congregation took their seats. Then, at the scheduled time, Spurgeon would ascend the stairs to the platform along with the other church officers. As they took their seats, the congregation grew quiet. There would be a pause for silent prayer. Spurgeon encouraged his students not to feel the need to fill every moment with sound. "It will frequently be a most profitable thing to let the people sit quite still in profound silence for two or five minutes. Solemn silence makes noble worship."[28] After a moment, Spurgeon would rise and begin

---

[28] *Lectures* 1:69.

the service with the simple phrase, "Brethren, let us pray." This opening prayer would typically be a prayer of praise and invocation.

The second prayer was the pastoral prayer. This was a longer prayer, usually 10 to 15 minutes, sometimes longer. These prayers included themes of praise, confession, thanksgiving, and supplication. Records show that Spurgeon always prayed in the first-person plural. Even as he spoke to God, he never forgot about his congregation. While he was careful not to "go into every minute detail of the circumstances of the congregation,"[29] yet he sought to pray about the real challenges and temptations that they faced.

Spurgeon's prayers were always delivered extemporaneously. Still, they evidenced careful thought and preparation. He counseled his students against using written prayers (like the liturgy of the Church of England), because that tended toward prayers being *read*, rather than *prayed*. However, he also warned against rambling, pointless prayers, but encouraged them to prepare to pray, perhaps even more than they prepared to preach.[30] After all, prayer was not about a performance but communing with the living God. As for Spurgeon, he confessed at times being so absorbed in prayer and adoration, "that he has quite forgotten all his surroundings, and has felt even a measure of regret, upon closing his petition, and opening his eyes, to find that he was still in the flesh, in the company of men of like passions with himself, instead of being in the immediate presence of the most High, sharing in the higher worship of the holy angels and the spirits of just men made perfect."[31]

There is not enough room in this chapter to include a transcript of one of Spurgeon's prayers, but here are excerpts from one of them, entitled "The Washing of Water by the Word." As you read

---

[29] *Lectures* 1:61.

[30] For more of Spurgeon's instructions to his students on praying, see *Lectures to My Students*, volume 1, lecture 4.

[31] *Autobiography* 4:71.

this, notice how boldly Spurgeon prays, how filled with Scripture his prayers are, and how earnestly he prays for his people.

> JEHOVAH, our God, Thou lovest Thy people, Thou hast placed all the saints in the hand of Jesus and Thou hast given Jesus to be to them a leader, a commander, and a husband and we know that Thou delightest to hear us cry on the behalf of Thy Church for Thou carest for Him and Thou art ready to grant to Him according to the covenant provisions which Thou hast laid up in store for Christ Jesus. Therefore, would we begin this prayer by entreating Thee to behold and visit the vine and the vineyard which Thy right hand hath planted. Look upon Zion the city of our solemnities. Look upon those whom Thou hast chosen from before the foundation of the world, whom Christ hath redeemed with blood, whose hearts He has won and holds, and who are His own though they be in the world.
>
> Holy Father, keep Thy people, we beseech Thee, for Jesus' sake Though they are in the world, let them not be of it, but may there be a marked distinction between them and the rest of mankind. Even as their Lord was holy, harmless, and undefiled, and separate from sinners, so may it be with believers in Christ. May they follow Him and may they not know the voice of strangers, but come out from the rest that they may follow Him without the camp.
>
> We cry to Thee for the preservation of Thy Church in the world and especially for her purity. O Father, keep us, we beseech Thee with all

keeping, that the evil one touch us not. We shall be tempted, but let him not prevail against us. In a thousand ways, he will lay snares for our feet, but oh! Deliver us as a bird from the snare of the fowler. May the snare be broken that we may escape. Let not Thy Church suffer dishonor at any time, but may her garments be always white. Let not such as come in among her that are not of her utterly despoil her. O Christ, as Thou didst groan concerning Judas, so may Thy children cry to Thee concerning any that have fallen aside into crooked ways, lest the cause of Christ in the earth should be dishonored. O God, cover, we beseech Thee, with Thy feathers all the people of Christ and keep Thy Church even until He shall come Who, having loved His own that were in the world, loveth them even to the end. . . .

Now we would bring before Thee all Thy saints and ask Thee to attend to their trials and troubles. Some we know are afflicted in person, others are afflicted in their dear friends, some are afflicted in their temporal estate and are brought into sore distress. Lord, we do not know the trials of all Thy people, but Thou dost, for Thou are the Head, and the pains of all the members are centered in Thee. Help all Thy people even to the end.

Now we pray Thee to grant us the blessing which we have already sought and let it come upon all the churches of our beloved country. May the Lord revive true and undefiled religion here and in all the other lands where Christ is known and preached, and let the day come when heathendom shall become converted, when the crescent of Mohammed shall wane into eternal night, and when she that sitteth on the Seven Hills and exalteth herself in the place of God shall be cast down to sink like a millstone in the flood.

Let the blessed Gospel of the eternal God prevail, let the whole earth be filled with His glory. Oh! That we may live to see that day. The Lord bless our country. Have pity upon it. God bless the Sovereign with every mercy and blessing. Grant that there may be in Thine infinite wisdom a change in the state of trade and commerce, that there may be less complaint and distress. Oh! Let the people see Thy hand and understand why it is laid upon them, that they may turn from wrongdoing, and seek righteousness and follow after peace. Then shall the blessing return. The Lord hear us as in secret we often cry to Thee on behalf of this misled land. The Lord deliver it and lift up the light of His countenance upon it yet again, for Jesus' sake. Amen.[32]

Scripture Readings

In preparation for preaching the Word, Spurgeon always selected a Scripture reading related to his sermon text. This reading would always be a longer passage of Scripture, usually a chapter or so, and would be accompanied by his own commentary to help his people understand what they heard. Spurgeon emphasized the importance of Scripture reading (or Scripture expositions, as he called them) in the service. While sermons did not always have to

---

[32] C. H. Spurgeon, *The Pastor in Prayer* (Edinburgh: Banner of Truth, 2004), 87.

be expositional, the people were always taught to be rooted in God's Word in these readings.

Often, his goal in these readings was to expose his people to the wider context of his sermon passage. Because he usually preached on single verses, his Scripture readings helped his people gain a broader view of the Bible. "The present plan of preaching from short texts, together with the great neglect of commenting publicly upon the Word is very unsatisfactory. We cannot expect to deliver much of the teaching of Holy Scripture by picking out verse by verse, and holding these up at random."[33]

These Scripture readings were also helpful in introducing and exposing his people to difficult parts of the Bible. Spurgeon encouraged his students to read from the whole Bible, and not to avoid difficult passages. "We must make sure in our public expositions that obscure and involved sentences are explained. To overleap difficulties, and only expound what is already clear, is to make commenting ridiculous."[34] The passages which troubled them were likely also the ones that troubled the congregation. The pastor had to be ready to explain those difficulties. As his members understood their Bibles better, they would be better equipped to lead their families in Bible reading and worship at home.

At the same time, Spurgeon did not wish to turn expositions into academic exercises. He warned his students against delving into fanciful interpretations or novel theologies. Though his students had studied Hebrew and Greek, he warned them against needlessly pointing out errors in the English translation. Such "vainglorious display of your critical ability" would only cause the people to mistrust the only Bible they could read.[35]

---

[33] *Lectures* 4:31.
[34] *Lectures* 4:28.
[35] *Lectures* 4:31.

Most of all, the pastor should apply the Scripture text to his hearers. "The chief part of your commenting, however, should consist in applying the truth to the hearts of your hearers . . . it is of little service to supply men with information unless we urge upon them the practical inferences therefrom."[36] In modeling regular Scripture reading and commenting, the pastor not only taught his people the Scriptures, but he trained them to read the Bible for themselves.

Congregational Singing

Spurgeon always arrived early before the service to coordinate with the song leader (also known as precentor) on the hymns and tunes for the service. The hymns and tunes were chosen based on two criteria. First, they were chosen according to the themes of the Scripture text and sermon. Prior to 1866, the church used two different hymnals, "Dr. Rippon's Selection" and "Dr. Watts' Psalms and Hymns." But after watching visitors fumble with two different hymnals, Spurgeon compiled his own hymnal, *Our Own Hymnbook*, filled with hymns that gave expression to the church's theological convictions and drew from a wide range of traditions. When picking songs to correspond with a particular text or theme, Spurgeon had a large, curated selection of hymns from which to choose.

In addition to theological content, congregational singing was the other top priority when it came to the music of the church. Spurgeon picked hymns and tunes that his congregation sang well and avoided those that provided struggles. Because of this priority, there were no instruments in his worship services. That's not to say he didn't enjoy instrumental music. They had their place in other venues, even religious venues. But when it came to the worship gathering, Spurgeon believed that musical instruments were often a distraction or hindrance to congregational singing. The

---

[36] *Lectures* 4:29.

best musical accompaniment was inferior to the beauty of the singing of the saints. "There can be no music under heaven that can
equal the combination of voices which belong to men, women, and
children whose hearts really love the Savior."[37] In other words, his
choice of acapella singing was driven not so much by a low view of
instruments, but a high view of the church. For that same reason,
Spurgeon also refused to have choirs. Again, they tended to distract, rather than enhance, the church's singing. Instead, Spurgeon
taught that the congregation was to be the choir, singing their
praises to an audience of One.

To help them in that task, Spurgeon encouraged his precentor to organize singing classes during the week to teach members
to read music and memorize hymn tunes. When trying out new
hymns and tunes, Spurgeon attempted them first at a smaller weeknight service. Only if the congregation sang them well, would he
bring those hymns and tunes to the larger Sunday services. During
the service, to help his people not only sing, but sing *intelligently*,
Spurgeon read through the entire hymn so that the congregation
could reflect on what they were about to sing. This may sound wearisome, but at least one visitor reported being converted as Spurgeon
read out Wesley's hymn, "Jesus, Lover of My Soul."

Once the hymn was properly introduced, then, following
the precentor, the congregation would rise to sing, "as only a
Tabernacle audience of six thousand people could sing."[38] Indeed,
the Metropolitan Tabernacle was known throughout London for
their singing. One visitor in 1880 reports,

> As the people stood up the precentor advanced
> from the back of the platform and started the
> melody with a clear voice. Like a giant that needs

---

[37] *MTP* 49:458.
[38] *Autobiography* 4:22.

a moment to arouse himself the congregation allowed a note or two to pass before they entered in full strength. Then the heavy tide of sound streamed forth from every part of the building. Many churches have more cultivated congregational singing than Mr. Spurgeon's, but, from the numbers engaged, no other singing touches the heart with such an indefinable pleasure, and makes the frame glow with such a sense of worshipful sympathy.[39]

Another visitor in 1868 who hadn't heard of Spurgeon but was encouraged to visit the Tabernacle wrote to her friend, "You would like to hear all the people sing together, Susie; for they sing as though they enjoyed it. I liked it better than I did the music in the Abbey, for at Mr. Spurgeon's church I could sing, too."[40]

For all the practical things that he did to help his people's singing, Spurgeon found that the most important factor was not musical skill, but the heart. As a result, singing would often improve as the service went along and the people responded to God's Word in praise. If you want to improve your congregation's voices, then warm their hearts with the truth of the gospel. "If you cannot sing artistically, never mind, you will be right enough if you sing from the heart, and pay attention to it, and do not drawl out like a musical machine that has been set therefore runs on mechanically. With a little care the heart brings the art, and the heart desiring to praise will by-and-by train the voice to time and tune."[41]

---

[39] J. Spencer Curwen, *Studies in Worship-Music, Chiefly as Regards Congregational Singing* (London: J. Curwen & Sons, 1880), 208.

[40] W. L. Gage, *Helen on Her Travels: What She Saw and What She Did in Europe* (Hurd & Houghton, New York: 1868), 48.

[41] *MTP* 14:141.

Conclusion

Today, the gathering of the church is under attack. In many parts of the world persecution and government interference threaten the ability of Christians to gather. Such challenges require much wisdom and courage. However, in places where there is religious liberty, internal factors also threaten the gathering of the church. In some ways, these challenges are even more concerning. Consumerism has turned church services into a shopping mall, preventing the entire church from ever gathering. Technology now allows Christians to "attend" services from their living room. Parachurch Bible studies, support groups, and service ministries are all marketed as alternatives to the gathering of the church. Like every age of church history, Christians are tempted to forsake assembling with other believers.

But Spurgeon would remind us of the apostles' command to the church to gather on the Lord's Day for worship. Spurgeon would remind us that the gathering of the church comes with Christ's promise of His special presence, that the church is to be governed by the Word of Christ, and that in the gathering of the church, Christ's reign is proclaimed and displayed.

Pastors, give your people a theological vision for the gathering of the church. Organize the ministries and activities of the church in a way that prioritizes the worship gathering. Keep the elements of the service simple and spiritually edifying to the congregation. And disciple your people to prioritize the church's gathering over other competing interests. As you pursue faithfulness in your church's gatherings, may the communion of saints here on earth become "the very gate of heaven."

3

TOKENS OF UNITY

BAPTISM AND THE
LORD'S SUPPER

Becoming a Baptist

It was an Anglican priest that pushed Spurgeon toward becoming a Baptist. (I wonder if fellow clergymen ever gave that priest a hard time in future years?) Born into a Congregationalist family, Spurgeon was baptized as an infant by his grandfather. But as a child, Spurgeon often puzzled over the practice. To him, the baptismal basin looked more like a punch bowl. He heard of some who had qualms about infant baptism and were baptized as believers quietly at some other chapel. On one occasion, he saw a sick infant rushed to be baptized, which he found strange. As he got older and learned a little Greek, he could not find the word *baptizo* to mean sprinkle. Despite his questions, however, it was no small thing for him to contradict his family on this issue. If his grandfather and parents believed in infant baptism, who was he to disagree? Spurgeon was content to leave the issue alone. That is, until this Anglican priest came along.

When he was fourteen, Spurgeon was sent to St. Augustine's College, Maidstone, a Church of England school where his uncle served as the headmaster. Spurgeon was bright and a bit cheeky at times. Perhaps to put this know-it-all dissenter in his place, one of the priests tested Spurgeon on baptism from the Church's catechism: "What is required of persons to be baptized?" Spurgeon knew the answer: "Repentance, whereby they forsake sin; and faith, whereby they steadfastly believe the promises of God made to them in that sacrament."

Because repentance and faith are necessary for baptism, the Church of England required sponsors to make promises on behalf of the infant, a practice not required by Congregationalists. The priest concluded, "Now, Charles, I shall give you till next week to find out whether the Bible does not declare faith and repentance to be necessary qualifications before baptism." Spurgeon went away looking for infant baptism in his New Testament but could not find it. "I was beaten," he confessed, "and made up my mind as to the course I would take . . . I resolved, from that moment, that if ever Divine grace should work a change in me, I would be baptized."[1] Spurgeon became convinced of the Baptist position.

In the spring of 1850, after his conversion, Spurgeon joined the Congregationalist church in Newmarket (there was no Baptist church in town). Whereas previously he had been content just to attend, Spurgeon now looked forward to full participation in the church. This, however, created a dilemma. The church accepted him into membership by virtue of his baptism as an infant. They now expected him to participate in the Lord's Supper. But Spurgeon no longer found his infant baptism valid. Like Christians before him, he understood that the New Testament required baptism as a prerequisite to participation in the Lord's Supper. Therefore, being unbaptized, Spurgeon refrained from the Table to the surprise of the pastor and other church members![2]

---

[1] *Autobiography* 1:49–50.

[2] Writing to his father, Spurgeon confessed, "Owing to my scruples on account of baptism, I did not sit down at the Lord's table, and cannot in conscience do so until I am baptized. To one who does not see the necessity of baptism, it is perfectly right and proper to partake of this blessed privilege; but were I to do so,

So, after joining the church, Spurgeon set about finding a Baptist minister. W. H. Cantlow was a classmate of Spurgeon's at Newmarket and his father, W. W. Cantlow, was the nearest Baptist minister, serving in Isleham. Through that connection, Spurgeon made the necessary arrangements for baptism. From the correspondence we have leading up to his baptism, it appears that Spurgeon's father didn't entirely approve and kept him in suspense waiting for his approval. Certainly, Spurgeon believed baptism to be a matter of obedience to Christ, but at the same time, he did not wish to dishonor his parents. His father did finally give permission, though Spurgeon recalls that "he [was] rather hard upon me."

So, on May 3, 1850, Spurgeon and W. H. Cantlow walked the eight miles from Newmarket to the River Lark and was baptized. He writes,

> My timidity was washed away; it floated down the river into the sea, and must have been devoured by the fishes, for I have never felt anything of the kind since. Baptism also loosed my tongue, and from that day it has never been quiet. I lost a thousand fears in that River Lark, and found that "in keeping His commandments there is great reward."[3]

On the following Lord's Day, May 5, Spurgeon participated in the Lord's supper for the first time, "This afternoon, partook of the Lord's supper; a royal feast for me, worthy of a King's son."[4]

In one sense, the decision to be baptized was not hard. Scripture was clear and Spurgeon resolved to obey. At the same time, this was a complicated decision. Coming from a Congregationalist family

---

I conceive would be to tumble over the wall, since I feel persuaded it is Christ's appointed way of professing Him." *Autobiography* 1:121.

[3] *Autobiography* 1:152.
[4] *Autobiography* 1:135.

and having joined a Congregationalist church, Spurgeon's conviction about believer's baptism would be tested. Would he commit himself to obeying Scripture even at the risk of being misunderstood and alienating his loved ones? Indeed, he would.

But for Spurgeon, this was no hardship. The ordinances were a source of joy. When his mother heard he had been baptized, she exclaimed, "Ah, Charles! I often prayed the Lord to make you a Christian, but I never asked that you might become a *Baptist*." Spurgeon famously responded, "Ah, mother! the Lord has answered your prayer with His usual bounty, and given you exceeding abundantly above what you asked or thought."[5]

In this chapter, we will explore Spurgeon's theology and practice of the ordinances, first considering baptism, then the Lord's Supper. In both ordinances, we will see that Spurgeon's practice was ordered by conviction, not convenience. While we may not agree with all of Spurgeon's positions, his example of faithfulness remains instructive to this day.

The Ordinances of the Church

Spurgeon held to two ordinances of the church: baptism and the Lord's Supper. He avoided the use of the term *sacrament*, which the Church of England defined as "an outward and visible sign of an inward and spiritual grace." He appreciated the idea of a visible sign. But at the same time, Spurgeon rejected any Roman Catholic understanding of the sacraments as meritorious apart from faith in Christ. This superstitious view continued at a popular level even among Protestants.

Therefore, Spurgeon preferred the term ordinance, which simply meant that baptism and the Lord's Supper were ordained

---

[5] *Autobiography* 1:69.

by Christ for the church. Because they were given by Christ, His Word is to govern their practice. While faith was central to one's participation, Christians must also abide by the forms that we have been given. Even as churches grew more elaborate in their celebration of the ordinances, Spurgeon believed that simplicity was the most important quality. For Spurgeon, simplicity promoted faith. Through obedience and faith, the ordinances became a source of rich, personal communion with Christ.

Spurgeon's Baptismal Theology

What was Spurgeon's baptismal theology? Three points are worth highlighting. Firstly, Spurgeon rejected any salvific or meritorious understanding of baptism. Baptism was for those who had already been saved through repentance and faith in Christ, performed as an act of obedience. "Baptism is for saints, not for sinners; like the Lord's Supper, it is in the Church, not out of it. Believing you are saved. Baptism does not save you; you are baptized because you are saved."[6] To miss this point would be to miss the gospel.

One of the most significant controversies that Spurgeon sparked was the Baptismal Regeneration Controversy in 1864, attacking the growing influence of Roman Catholic theology in the Church of England. The sermon that started it all attacked the language of baptismal regeneration found in the Book of Common Prayer. Spurgeon believed that such language that declared baptized infants to be regenerate by virtue of their baptism was antithetical to the gospel. Such an understanding of baptism compromised the gospel in the Church of England, and Spurgeon called evangelicals to leave the Church. Spurgeon took baptism seriously and any salvific understanding of baptism effectively "unchurched" a church.

---

[6] *MTP* 9:24.

While baptism was not saving, Spurgeon viewed it as a matter of convictional obedience. Recounting his own experience of baptism, Spurgeon writes, "I did not fulfill the outward ordinance to join a party, and to become a Baptist, but to be a Christian after the apostolic fashion; for they, when they believed, were baptized."[7] When he became convinced of believer's baptism, Spurgeon didn't even know that Baptists existed as a denomination. As far as he was concerned, this was a matter of obedience to Scripture.

Therefore, those coming from a paedobaptist background and wanting to join the Tabernacle needed to be convinced from Scripture about believer's baptism. It was not sufficient for them to merely be willing to submit to the church's requirement of baptism. They had to do it out of conviction, otherwise they could not join the church.

Second, baptism was a mark of distinction between the world and the church. On the one hand, baptism pictured dying to the world. Spurgeon writes,

> Baptism is the mark of distinction between the Church and the world. It very beautifully sets forth the death of the baptized person to the world. Professedly, he is no longer of the world; he is buried to it, and he rises again to a new life. No symbol could be more significant. In the immersion of a believer, there seems to me to be a wondrous setting forth of the burial of the Christian to all the world in the burial of Christ Jesus.[8]

Baptism also united the believer to the church. This relationship was pictured in church membership. Spurgeon always held baptism and church membership together. In the thousands who

---

[7] *Autobiography* 1:154.
[8] *Autobiography* 1:149–50.

were baptized at the Metropolitan Tabernacle, all of them were brought into church membership. As the initiatory ordinance of the church, baptism was "necessary to the very existence of the Church of God" because this is the way Christians were brought into the church.[9]

Finally, Spurgeon believed that baptism pictured the Christian's union with Christ in His death and resurrection.[10] In one's own baptism and in every baptismal service in the church, the Christian was reminded of his union with Christ. Thus, baptism became a wonderful expression of the believer's faith. While Spurgeon rejected baptism as being in any way salvific, he held faith and baptism closely together. All those who have genuine saving faith in Christ should and will want to express it by being baptized. "Baptism is the outward expression of your faith. You are immersed in water to signify that you believe that you are buried with Christ, and that you rise again to life in him. But the saving matter is the believing—the trusting is the great soul-saving grace."[11] Therefore, like the apostles, Spurgeon did not hesitate to call people to respond to the gospel by believing and being baptized.[12]

For those who have been united to Christ in His death, they are also raised to walk in newness of life. In baptism, the Christian proclaims that he is dead to sin and alive to God. With this ordinance at the beginning of the Christian life, the clear expectation is holy

---

[9] *MTP* 39:607.

[10] "As a believer he is buried, and is that watery sign of baptism mine? Yes, 'Buried with Christ in baptism unto death.' Jesus' baptism I share when I lie interred with my best friend in the selfsame watery tomb. See there he dies, and it is a master work to die. But is his death mine? Yes, I die in Christ. He is buried, and is that burial mine? Yes, I am buried with Christ. He rises. Mark him startling his guards, and rising from the tomb! And is that resurrection mine? Yes, we are 'risen together with Christ.'" *NPSP* 2:395.

[11] *MTP* 13:778.

[12] Cf. Acts 2:38; Spurgeon also often quoted from Mark 16:16, a text which is not found in the earliest manuscripts.

living. "Thus, at the very doorstep of the Christian religion, in its first inward act and its first outward symbol, you get the thought that believers are henceforth to be separated from sin and purified in life."[13]

Spurgeon's Baptismal Practice

As important as baptism was, Spurgeon rarely preached directly on the topic. Of course, his sermons often included baptism as an illustration or a theological truth or a point of application. But out of his 3,563 published sermons, only ten of them are topical sermons devoted to baptism. His mission was not to convert people to believer's baptism, but to Jesus Christ. On one occasion, he was invited to preach in Ireland to further the cause of Baptists there. Spurgeon responded, "No, I would not go across the street, much less across the sea, merely to make people Baptists. Wherever I may be, I endeavor, as in the sight of God, so to deal with men as to bring them to Christ, leaving the Spirit of God further to take of the things of Christ, and reveal them unto them."[14]

Even so, thousands of those who were baptized at the Metropolitan Tabernacle came from paedobaptist backgrounds. Spurgeon's strategy for persuading these people was simply to encourage them to study the New Testament for themselves. "Of those who have come to unite with us in church-fellowship, a very large proportion consists of persons who have searched out the truth upon this matter for themselves, and could in no wise trace their alteration in sentiment to any remark of mine, but they had seen the ordinance clearly revealed in Holy Scripture."[15]

---

[13] *MTP* 21:341.
[14] *MTP* 47:349.
[15] *MTP* 47:349.

Even if Spurgeon did not dwell on believer's baptism in preaching, he also did not hide his convictions. This was clear even in the church's architecture. The Metropolitan Tabernacle was built with a massive marble baptistry on the front platform, one that Spurgeon hoped would last "at least until Christ should come a second time." This baptistry was permanently fixed into the lower platform, in full view of the entire auditorium. On any given Sunday, the baptistry was uncovered and filled with water for all to see, even if no one was scheduled to be baptized! On one occasion, Spurgeon was sharing the platform with other paedobaptist ministers, and he commented that if the platform were to give way, all those on it would find themselves in the baptistry. In that case, he would be glad to immerse any of them that needed to be baptized. The church was not ashamed to avow their belief in believer's baptism and the baptistry stood as a symbol of their convictions and a call for sinners to follow Christ.

Fencing the Baptismal Pool

Just because the baptistry was always uncovered and filled doesn't mean Spurgeon baptized people carelessly. He would have repudiated the modern practice of spontaneous baptism. While the baptismal pool stood as an invitation to sinners, there was still a process for baptism. He writes, "as the communion table should be fenced, so also should the baptismal pool, so should the promises of God, and so should those great and glorious doctrines which are the essentials of our faith."[16] Hypocrites who rushed to be baptized were immersed to their own condemnation.

The fencing of the baptismal pool involved a rigorous membership process, which was necessary in a Christianized society like nineteenth-century London. Because Spurgeon held baptism and

---

[16] *MTP* 47:350.

church membership together, the process for being baptized at the Metropolitan Tabernacle was the same as joining the church. Only after having been interviewed by the elders and approved by the congregation, was a convert eligible for baptism. The purpose was not to needlessly delay baptism. Spurgeon did not require lengthy classes or catechetical instruction. Rather, the only prerequisite to baptism was a credible profession of faith. This is what the membership process helped to discern. Did the individual give credible evidence to believing in Christ with all his heart and would they commit to joining the church? If so, they would be baptized as soon as possible.

Age of Baptism

Spurgeon set no age requirement for baptism. "We do not contend for baptism of adults; we contend for the baptism of believers. Show us a child however young, who believes in Christ, and we gladly accept him."[17] For all youths who were baptized, they went through the same membership process as every other member of the church, including interviews with the pastor and the elders about their faith.[18] Spurgeon refused to separate baptism from church membership. Upon their baptism, all candidates would become members of the church and would be subject to the accountability and discipline of the church.

One example of a young baptismal candidate comes from 1856, when Spurgeon baptized Alfred Moore, the ten-year-old son of one of his deacons.[19] But Alfred was not admitted simply by virtue of his dad's position. The minute books show that Deacon Moore was

---

[17] *MTP* 7:266.

[18] See chapter 4 for the membership process at the Metropolitan Tabernacle.

[19] "Denominational Intelligence—Baptism," *The Baptist Messenger: An Evangelical Treasury and Chronicle of the Churches from January to June, 1856 with Portraits of Ten Baptist Ministers*. Magazine D (London: James Paul, 1856), 72.

not involved in his son's membership process, but rather it was conducted by Spurgeon and the other deacons. Spurgeon did not simplify the membership process for younger applicants but tested each youth's understanding of the gospel and experience of grace.[20] In interviewing children for membership, Spurgeon once reported, "I was delighted to hear them, one after another, not only express themselves clearly upon the great fundamental truth of justification by faith, but also give clear evidence that they were well instructed in the doctrines that cluster around the covenant of grace."[21]

At the same time, Spurgeon instructed parents not to pressure their children to baptism. "I do not know that the parent needs to say much to his child about baptism or the Lord's Supper, except, sometimes, a gentle word as to the duty of the believer, and a clear explanation of the meaning of the ordinances."[22] Instead, the primary task of the parents was to pray for their salvation and teach the gospel. He cautioned them from ever assuming that their children were good boys and girls, who could reach heaven through good behavior. Rather, parents were to know that their children are spiritually dead by nature and in need of the saving work of the Spirit. Yet parents could hope and pray that God, in His grace, might work powerfully through their teaching and prayers for the salvation of their children.

---

[20] For a few examples of youth baptized at New Park Street Chapel and their membership interviews, see Hannah Wyncoll, ed., *Wonders of Grace: Original Testimonies of Converts during Spurgeon's Early Years* (London: The Wakeman Trust, 2016). One example is Clara Rayment, aged fourteen. The interviewing elder concludes with these comments, "This is a most pleasing case. Her sensitivity is manifested when I touched upon sin and repentance, and especially when I asked her concerning any besetting sin—which she acknowledged to be hastiness of temper—showed to me her sincerity of heart. I put many puzzling questions to her, all of which she answered readily and to the purpose. Her doctrinal knowledge is good. Gave a card with extreme pleasure." Wyncoll, *Wonders of Grace*, 72.

[21] *Autobiography* 2:224–25.

[22] *MTP* 10:564.

In the case of his own twin boys, Spurgeon had the joy of seeing them make a profession of faith at an early age. Thomas Spurgeon tells the story of climbing into his mother's lap as a young boy and confessing his love for Christ. Rather than doubting him, Susannah responded, "I am so glad to hear it, I believe you do." Thomas remembers being so glad that she took him at his word.[23] But even so, the Spurgeons did not baptize them right away. Instead, they continued to encourage them in their faith. Throughout their teenage years, Charles Jr. and Thomas were involved with the youth group at the Tabernacle. They were known as Christians in their school, participated in evangelistic outreach, and more. Letters from their parents during these years reveal their parental affection and their encouragement for their sons to persevere in faith. Finally, on September 20, 1874, their eighteenth birthday, Charles Jr. and Thomas were baptized by their father and joined the Metropolitan Tabernacle. Though Spurgeon was willing to baptize and bring children into membership, when it came to his own boys, he took a more patient approach and waited until they were older.

The Baptism Service

What was it like to be baptized at the Tabernacle during those days? Spurgeon only baptized in the context of a public gathering of the church. Baptismal services were normally held during the week, usually at the Monday or Thursday night service. Like all services, members and visitors were welcome. The service included all the typical elements of a worship gathering: prayer, singing, Scripture reading, and a sermon, usually containing words of exhortation for the baptismal candidates. Then, at the conclusion of the service, baptismal candidates came forward and were baptized in the name

---

[23] W. Y. Fullerton, *Thomas Spurgeon: A Biography* (London: Hodder and Stoughton, 1919), 36.

of the Father, Son, and Holy Ghost by the pastor or another officer of the church.

In the archives of the Tabernacle, there is a letter that was sent to Elizabeth Broomfield with instructions for her baptism on Thursday, February 19, 1891. Elizabeth should arrive no later than five o'clock (remember, the Thursday night service starts at seven), "in order that there may be no hurry and confusion, but a little time for quiet prayer before the Service." Because of the many attendants and candidates present, there would be no room for friends and family, so she should come alone. The church would provide a white cap and dress "for uniformity of appearance" and Elizabeth was welcome to contribute a voluntary donation of two shillings, or more, to help with the upkeep of these articles (which apparently saw a lot of use!). Underneath the white dress, Elizabeth should bring the following articles of clothing to wear:

White Gloves.

Black Shoes (without heels) or Goloshes . . .

Stays.

A white Skirt.

A pair of white Stockings.

And a complete change of Underclothing.

(N. B. Scarlet flannel must not be worn in any case.)

The letter states that these articles were "all absolutely necessary, and it is most inconvenient for friends to come without them."[24] By 1891, having baptized so many and learned from their mistakes, the process was designed to care for each candidate and ensure the process went smoothly. But more than just efficiency, we see in these instructions an intentionality. From the marble baptistry down to the white clothing worn by each candidate, baptism provided a visual reminder that our scarlet sins have been washed white through the blood of Christ.

Spurgeon's Communion Theology

When Spurgeon moved to Cambridge in the summer 1850, he joined St. Andrew's Street Baptist Church. In one of his first communion services there, nobody spoke to him. But Spurgeon believed that the Table signified spiritual fellowship, so he struck up a conversation with the person sitting next to him. This would lead to a lifelong friendship.[25] In future years, these two would look back on this event "and laugh at the fact that I should have dared to assume that Christian fellowship was really a truth."

Spurgeon believed that Christian fellowship was really a truth. It was no invention of man or idealistic dream. No, through the gospel, God's people have been united to the Son and adopted into the family of God. Through the gospel, the church is the body of

---

[24] Baptism Instructions for Elizabeth Broomfield, February 17, 1891, Metropolitan Tabernacle Archives, London.

[25] "'I hope you are quite well, sir?' He said, 'You have the advantage of me.' I answered, 'I don't think I have, for you and I are brothers.' 'I don't quite know what you mean,' said he. 'Well,' I replied, 'when I took the bread and wine, just now, in token of our being one in Christ, I meant it, did not you?' We were by that time in the street; he put both his hands on my shoulders,—was about sixteen years old then,—and he said, 'Oh, sweet simplicity!' Then he added, 'You are quite right, my dear brother, you are quite right; come in to tea with me. I am afraid I should not have spoken to you if you had not first addressed me.'" *Autobiography* 1:185.

Christ and Christians are members of it. And the expression of this fellowship is found in the Lord's Supper.

Spurgeon's theology of the Lord's Supper stood within the Reformed tradition. Unlike baptism, he preached many sermons about the significance of the Lord's Supper.[26] Much could be said about his communion theology, but let me highlight three points. First, he held to a memorialist position. The communion table was an opportunity for Christians to remember Christ's broken body and shed blood for their sins. The best way to remember Christ was not by trying to bring something to the Table, but by receiving his finished work by faith.[27]

As a memorialist, Spurgeon did not want his people to remember Christ abstractly or academically. He urged his people to remember Christ *personally*. Preaching on Luke 22:19, Spurgeon declared, "The pith and essence of your business at his table is, 'This do in remembrance of me,' that is, of himself—of his own blessed person."[28] It is Christ that we are to remember, not a doctrine, or a theological truth, or a promise, but Christ himself. In that, Spurgeon's memorialist position blended with a strong belief in the spiritual presence of Christ at the Table.

This brings us to the second aspect of Spurgeon's communion theology, namely that in the Lord's Supper, Christians commune

---

[26] For a whole volume of his communion sermons, see Charles H. Spurgeon, *"Till He Come:" Communion Meditations and Addresses* (Pasadena, TX: Pilgrim, 1971).

[27] "You are taught by this institution that the very best way in which you can remember Christ is by receiving him. Oh the sweetness of that truth if you will remember it when you come to this table! You are not asked to bring bread with you. It is here. You are not asked to bring a cup with you. It is here already provided. What have you to do? Nothing but to eat, and to drink. You have to be receivers, and nothing more. Well, now, whenever you want to remember your Lord and Master, you need not say, 'I must do something for him.' No, no, let him do something for you. 'Take the cup of salvation, and call upon the name of the Lord.'" *MTP* 34:453.

[28] *MTP* 34:448.

with Christ by faith. Spurgeon repudiated the Roman Catholic doctrine of transubstantiation for how it minimized Christ's finished
work on the cross. Christ's physical presence was not at the Table
but at the right hand of the Father in heaven. Spurgeon did believe,
however, in Christ's spiritual presence with His people, which could
be grasped by faith especially at the Lord's Supper.[29] It is no surprise, then, that many of Spurgeon's communion devotions are
taken from the Song of Songs, meditating on Christ's communion
with the church, his bride. By faith, the elements of the bread and
the cup became tokens of His presence with His people, for their
joy and comfort.

Third, Spurgeon understood the Lord's Supper to be a meal
for the church. Just as the baptistry was reserved for believers, so
also the Table. In the one loaf and one cup, in the use of a table, in
the acts of giving and receiving, the Lord's Supper was filled with
symbols of the church's unity and fellowship with one another. In
a gathering where hundreds of visitors, maybe thousands, mixed in
among the members of the church, Spurgeon was concerned that
unbelievers might partake of the Table and bring judgment upon
themselves. The elders had to carefully consider how to fence the
Table appropriately so that their celebration might continue to be a
visible expression of the fellowship within the church.

Spurgeon's Communion Practice

When Spurgeon first arrived at the New Park Street Chapel, the
congregation numbered a few dozen and the building seated a thousand. Soon, however, the membership grew and visitors poured into

---

[29] "The provision is but bread and wine; but when, by faith, we perceive the
real and spiritual presence of the Lord Jesus Christ, in the breaking of the bread
we eat his flesh, and in the fruit of the vine we drink his blood. . . . At the Master's
table I have often been so blest that I would not have exchanged places with
Gabriel. The Lord was there: what more could I desire?" *MTP* 37:9.

the services. It became harder and harder to find room for everyone. To accommodate the growing crowds, Spurgeon reserved larger venues like Exeter Hall and Surrey Gardens Music Hall for Sunday morning services but returned to his own chapel for Sunday evening services. Even then, people were still being turned away.

As an evangelist, Spurgeon mourned to see unbelievers turned away. But as a pastor, Spurgeon was concerned that the church was not being cared for well. Given what the Lord's Supper represented, it was particularly painful that all members could not gather to take the Lord's Supper. Spurgeon recounted, "Indeed, we have 300 more friends, whose names are on the church-book, than are able to sit down in the area of the chapel to partake of the communion." The church made temporary accommodations, like adding a second communion service in the month so that everyone could participate over two weeks. But this was not enough.

Spurgeon's passion was seeing the lost saved *and* the church nurtured. Given the space issues, he felt that he could not do either adequately. He writes, "I made up my mind that either a suitable place must be built, or I would resign my pastorate . . . either the Tabernacle must be erected, or I would become an evangelist."[30] Spurgeon took the Lord's Supper so seriously that it almost forced him to resign his pastorate. The congregation, however, would not let him resign. They approved the construction of the Metropolitan Tabernacle. With the construction of this magnificent building in 1861, the church finally had a home where they could regularly partake of the Lord's Supper all together.

What were the distinctive features of Spurgeon's communion practice?

---

[30] *Autobiography* 2:313.

Frequency

The first one is frequency. Spurgeon believed that the New Testament provided a model for the frequent celebration of communion.[31] When he first arrived, the church celebrated the Lord's Supper once a month. Within a few years, they moved to twice a month to accommodate church growth. After the construction of the Tabernacle in 1861, the church had enough room to take the Lord's Supper all together in one service. But even so, Spurgeon's desire for the church to take the Lord's Supper frequently would grow, and he was not alone. In the minute books of the church, we see the following motion passed on October 8, 1863:

> Our Pastor stated that several of the brethren thought it their duty to celebrate the Lord's Supper every Sabbath, and he himself considered it to be an apostolic practice which ought to be revived. Although there is no express command for weekly communion yet it is certain that in the time of the apostles it was so observed, and therefore the Church agreed that convenience should be provided for those who desire it.[32]

From that point, the church celebrated the Lord's Supper weekly. Note that the motion above did not make attendance at every communion a matter of discipline. Rather, members viewed each Lord's Supper service differently. The first Sunday communion was still the most important one, known as "the great communion of

---

[31] "But, next, our Lord's Supper was intended to be very frequent. 'This do ye, as oft as ye drink it, in remembrance of me.' He has laid down no rule as to when we shall break bread; but the custom was certainly to break it on the first day of the week, and I think oftener, for it seems to me that they broke bread from house to house." *MTP* 34:451.

[32] Church Meeting October 8, 1863, *Church Meeting Minutes 1861–1866*, Metropolitan Tabernacle, Metropolitan Tabernacle Archives, London.

the Tabernacle." Like most other weeks, it was celebrated after the evening service (that service typically had less visitors). If you could only attend communion once a month, this was the one to attend. Members made a particular effort to be present for that celebration.

On the second Sunday of the month, the Lord's Supper was celebrated after the morning service to accommodate members who could not make it to an evening service. The members who served in Sunday schools, evangelistic missions, or other Sunday ministries participated in this one. On the third and fourth Sundays, the Lord's Supper was provided after the Sunday evening service "for those who desired it." Spurgeon presided and participated in all services.

Another aspect of the frequency of the Lord's Supper is that Spurgeon encouraged his members to take communion in smaller groups together with one another, even outside an official gathering of the church. "More than fifty-two times in the year is this table spread in our midst; for, frequently, in different parts of the Tabernacle, the elders and deacons and other friends meet, and commune with the Lord, doing this often in remembrance of him."[33] Certainly, Spurgeon would have expected that those partaking of the Table were all church members in good standing. Someone under church discipline should not be admitted to the Table. It's possible that Spurgeon may have also preferred an elder or deacon to be present. It's hard to know what these smaller occasions of the Lord's Supper were like and how discipline was enforced. But Spurgeon encouraged his people to partake of the Table frequently.[34]

---

[33] *MTP* 38:594.

[34] "It was not a ceremony that required a minister or a priest. When believers were together they broke bread in memory of Christ—any two or three of them— and so they remembered him. It is most delightful, when travelling, to remember Christ in your own room, where two or three brethren meet together. You have nothing to do but to break bread and drink wine in remembrance of him. I know of nothing more sweet or more instructive than this divine ordinance, which

Fencing

This brings us to another aspect of Spurgeon's communion practice, namely that it was fenced. Fencing is the practice of guarding the Lord's Table and reserving it for Christians only. It was not enough for any individual to privately profess their relationship with Christ. Rather, Spurgeon expected a profession of faith to be public, through baptism and membership in a local church. Otherwise, they could not participate at the Table.

Members of the Tabernacle in good standing, of course, were allowed to participate at the Table. With such a large membership, how could you know who was a member? Spurgeon adopted a Reformed practice, namely the use of communion tickets. At least twice a year, members were mailed a membership card that indicated their membership was in good standing and attached to the card would be six (or more) perforated communion tickets. Members bearing these tickets would be admitted to the Table.

Spurgeon, however, did not limit the Table to members only. Visitors were also allowed to participate. Early in his ministry, with so many visitors in attendance, Spurgeon learned of "certain unworthy persons having partaken of the Lord's Supper without their knowledge and consent, and that others whom they believe to be Christians but still are walking disorderly by not joining a Christian Church have also been partakers in this divine ordinance."[35] In response, the congregation approved a new policy that all visitors wanting to take communion would speak with a church elder ahead of time. During this interview, the elder would hear the person's testimony and their reason for taking the Lord's Supper at the Tabernacle, rather than at their own church. If all was in order, he

---

grows more impressive the oftener you attend to it. It ought to be frequent." *MTP* 34:541–42.

[35] Monthly Church Meeting August 13, 1856, *Church Minute Minutes 1854–1861 New Park Street*, Metropolitan Tabernacle Archives, London.

could grant communion tickets for the visitor, but for no more than three consecutive months.

Spurgeon held to an open communion position. This means that even though he believed that believer's baptism should precede communion, he would allow visitors who had only been sprinkled as infants to participate at the Table (as opposed to a strict communion position, which required all participants to have been baptized upon their profession of faith). His reasoning for this was that the Table pictured not only the believer's unity with the local church, but also with the universal church.[36] Any paedobaptist visitors who desired to partake of the Table needed to go through the interview process outlined above and be members in good standing of an evangelical church. For all such visitors, they were welcomed to the Table.

Beyond these practical methods, Spurgeon also fenced the Table verbally. As communion took place immediately following the service, Spurgeon often concluded his sermons by making clear who should participate. In such cases, he spoke particularly to the communicants seated in the main floor and first gallery of the church, where the Lord's Supper would soon be served. Even though they had their tickets, Spurgeon called each one of them to self-examination and warned them not to eat and drink judgment

---

[36] "At the Lord's table I always invite all Churches to come and sit down and commune with us. If any man were to tell me that I am separate from the Episcopalian, the Presbyterian, or the Methodist, I would tell him he did not know me, for I love them with a pure heart fervently, and I am not separate from them. I may hold different views from them, and in that point truly I may be said to be separate; but I am not separate in heart, I will work with them—I will work with them heartily. . . . Oh, how my heart loves the doctrine of the one church. The nearer I get to my Master in prayer and communion, the closer am I knit to all his disciples. The more I see of my own errors and failings, the more ready am I to deal gently with them that I believe to be erring. The pulse of Christ's body is communion; and woe to the church that seeks to cure the ills of Christ's body by stopping its pulse. I think it sin to refuse to commune with anyone who is a member of the Church of our Lord Jesus Christ." *NPSP* 4:23–24.

upon themselves. One example of this can be found in his sermon, "The Right Observance of the Lord's Supper,"

> If any of you, who have come to the table of the Lord, are not believers in Christ, never dare to come again while you are in that state. You have no right here unless you are resting in Jesus, and trusting in him. This is the proof of your being new creatures in Christ Jesus. But if you have the faintest, feeblest faith in Jesus, come and welcome. If you are trusting in your own merits, go to your own table; if you think there will be some merit in your coming to the communion, do not dare to come, for that were to turn the ordinance upside down.[37]

Even as the believer communed with Christ, he knew that he also communed with Christ's people. Because the elders did the work of fencing the Table, the people could come together with a clear conscience and joyfully proclaim their fellowship with those around them. Spurgeon encouraged his people to leave the work of fencing to the elders and embrace those sitting at the Table with them in the fellowship of the church.

> Some professedly Christian people urge that they cannot come to the table because there are certain persons there who, in their judgment, should not be allowed to come. Is the Lord's table to be a judgment-seat, whereat we are to revise the verdict of the church? . . .
>
> Surely this is the most unseasonable time for harsh judgments, or indeed for any judgments. I

---

[37] *MTP* 45:480.

know many a brother with whom I could not agree in certain points, but I agree with him in remembering the Lord Jesus. I could not work with him in all things; but if he wants to remember Jesus, I am sure I will join him in that. It will do him good, and it will do me good, to think of Jesus. That dear name is so sweet to me that I will remember Jesus with the poorest, meanest, and most imperfect of mortals.

I am never happier than when I am in your midst, my beloved brethren, and we all sit around the table, because I think of all the Lord has done for you and for me. Why, it is not going to heaven alone. A little lost child sits down on the doorstep of a West-end mansion and cries because it is so lonely is that to be our position in heaven? Are we to take no friends there with us? Who wants to be solitary in the New Jerusalem? But oh, to come with all of you to the table, and to look into the faces of all God's people, and to believe that the Lord Jesus Christ is in each one of them![38]

Even as Spurgeon encouraged his church to participate at the Table frequently, he also modeled the importance of fencing the Table. These values were held in tension. But rather than minimizing one or the other, Spurgeon promoted them both, in faithful obedience to the New Testament model.

Simplicity

Finally, Spurgeon cherished simplicity in the practice of the Lord's Supper. In one sense, there was nothing elaborate or

---

[38] *MTP* 34:455.

mysterious about the ordinance. Unlike those who found the New Testament model insufficient and "have added all kinds of rites and institutions," Spurgeon sought to preserve the simplicity that was given by Christ and the apostles. In that simplicity, he saw a reflection of Christ's humility.[39] Part of the simplicity can be seen in the elements themselves. Spurgeon used plain "household bread," not a wafer. When it came to the cup, Spurgeon emphasized that the cup should contain "the true juice of the grape, which our Lord called 'the fruit of the vine.'"[40] Spurgeon believed these were two distinct and necessary elements, and he did not approve of the mixing of the bread and the cup or withholding of either from the people.

The liturgy for the Lord's Supper was also very simple. At the conclusion of the Sunday service, those not participating in communion would be dismissed, unless they wanted to stay to observe. Most communicants would already be on the floor and first gallery to participate in the Lord's Supper. Deacons would collect tickets from all communicants. Then the elders would carry and distribute the elements on trays to all those participating. Once everyone was served, Spurgeon would invite everyone to take the elements in their hands and would speak the words of consecration, likely taken from 1 Corinthians 11 or one of the Gospels: "Whenever we break this bread, we say the same, 'This bread is Christ's body,' so there is an appeal to the ear."[41] Then together, they would partake of the bread and cup. After a moment, Spurgeon would lead in a prayer of thanksgiving, which was then followed by a joyful hymn, after the

---

[39] "But if you take the cloth from yonder table, you will see before you simply bread and wine; and when you see us celebrate the ordinance tonight, you will notice that we do nought but break the bread and eat it, and pass round the wine-cup and drink therefrom. All that is done is extremely simple; and the Savior seemed to wish for that simplicity, because he was himself a very simple, unaffected, plain man." *MTP* 34:450–51.

[40] *MTP* 39:221.

[41] *MTP* 39:222.

pattern of the Last Supper. Then, at the conclusion of the communion service, a collection would be taken "for the poor of the flock," allowing their communion to extend beyond their worship to their care for one another. The communion service normally lasted thirty minutes.

In the preaching of the Word, Spurgeon envisioned God assaulting our unbelief through the ear-gate (to use the image of Bunyan's *Holy War*). But in the bread and the cup, God waged war differently.[42] By being faithful to the simplicity of the Lord's Supper, Spurgeon allowed people to receive the gospel by their eyes, hands, and mouths, and, by faith, to grasp the spiritual realities that were pictured.

Conclusion

Many evangelical churches today struggle to know what to do with ordinances. They know it ought to be a part of the church, but there is little understanding of its theological meaning and the way it functions in the church's life. As a result, all kinds of dangerous innovations arise. Baptism ends up being spontaneous with little examination of those being baptized. The Lord's Supper is separated from the discipline of the church and becomes individualized. In all kinds of ways, as the church loses a biblical and theological understanding of the ordinances, the church is weakened, and the gospel is compromised.

---

[42] "He would not have us know him after the flesh, and forget the spiritual nature of his griefs; but yet he would have us know that he was in a real body when he bled, and that he died a real death, and became most truly fit for burial and therefore he symbolizes his blood, not by some airy fancy, or mystic sign, but by common wine in the cup. Thus would he reach us by our eye and by our taste, using two gates of our nature which lead up to the castle of the heart, but are not often the King's roadway thereto. O blessed Master, dost thou arrange to teach us so forcibly?" *MTP* 33:377.

Spurgeon, then, provides us a model for a convictional approach to the ordinances. That's not to say that there will never be tensions and difficulties in our practice. In cultures where nominal Christianity exists, amid church growth and discipline cases, pastors will need to give careful thought to fencing the ordinances. But in cultures where Christianity is persecuted, pastors will need to encourage converts to profess their faith and frequently remember Christ in the ordinances. These situations require much prayer and dependence on God and His Word for wisdom. But our confidence is that as we faithfully practice the ordinances, the church will be protected, and the gospel will be upheld.

4

A Hedging and Fencing
Regenerate Church Membership

Joining a Church

For four straight days, fifteen-year-old Spurgeon knocked on the door of the pastor of the Congregational chapel in Newmarket. And for four straight days, he was turned away. Spurgeon had been converted just a few weeks earlier, during the winter holidays of 1849–50. Now, he was back in Newmarket to finish his studies. But he wasn't thinking about school. He wanted to join the church. Writing to his mother in February, Spurgeon declared,

> I have come to a resolution that, by God's help, I will profess the name of Jesus as soon as possible if I may be admitted into His Church on earth. It is an honor,—no difficulty,—grandfather encourages me to do so, and I hope to do so both as a duty and privilege. I trust that I shall then feel that the bonds of the Lord are upon me, and have a more powerful sense of my duty to walk circumspectly.[1]

---

[1] *Autobiography* 1:119.

Still, joining the church in Newmarket would take perseverance. After being turned away four times, he chose to write a letter.
Spurgeon informed the pastor that if he didn't want to meet in person, then he would just show up at the next congregational meeting and propose himself for membership! Spurgeon recounts, "He
looked upon me as a strange character, but I meant what I said; for
I felt that I could not be happy without fellowship with the people
of God."[2]

It wasn't only the pastoral interview that was lacking. The
congregation also didn't think much about this new applicant.
Spurgeon was finally proposed for membership at a church meeting. This proposal lay over for a few weeks, giving church leaders
and the congregation a chance to get to know the applicant. But
writing to his father, Spurgeon expressed his disappointment, "At
our last church meeting, I was proposed. No one has been to see
me yet."[3] Evidently, Spurgeon had high hopes for the process of
joining the church. As a new Christian, he saw church membership as both duty and honor. But the Christians around him seemed
indifferent.

This, however, would not diminish Spurgeon's excitement. On
Thursday evening, April 4, 1850, he was officially voted in as a member of the Congregational church in Newmarket. He shared his joy
with his father a few days later,

> Since last Thursday, I have been unwell in body,
> but I may say that my soul has been almost in
> Heaven. I have been able to see my title clear, and
> to know and believe that, sooner than one of God's
> little ones shall perish, God Himself will *cease to
> be*, Satan will conquer the King of kings, and Jesus

---

[2] *Autobiography* 1:147.
[3] *Autobiography* 1:120.

will no longer be the Saviour of the elect. Doubts and fears may soon assail me, but I will not dread to meet them if my Father has so ordained it; He knows best.[4]

Spurgeon's confidence in God's sovereign grace was strengthened by his membership in the church. This would be a status he would maintain for the rest of his life.

For the next forty-two years, Spurgeon would be a member of four different churches:

- Congregational Church, Newmarket (April 4, 1850–October 2, 1850)
- St. Andrew's Street Baptist, Cambridge (October 2, 1850–October 26, 1851)
- Waterbeach Chapel (October 26, 1851–May 5, 1854)
- New Park Street Chapel / Metropolitan Tabernacle, London (May 5, 1854–January 31, 1892)

He could not envision following Christ apart from membership in the local church. Though his ministry would encompass the English-speaking world and beyond, Spurgeon would always remain rooted in the membership and accountability of a local church.

In this chapter, we will discuss Spurgeon's convictions regarding regenerate church membership and how he upheld those convictions through his membership process. With so many seeking membership, how did the church examine all of them? Let's find out.

---

[4] *Autobiography* 1:121.

Spurgeon's Teaching on Church Membership

Spurgeon's experience at Newmarket reveals something about his context. Being a member of a church was culturally expected. Writing in 1856, Spurgeon observed, "Religion has become fashionable. The shopkeeper could scarcely succeed in a respectable business if he were not united with a church. It is reckoned to be reputable and honorable to attend a place of worship."[5] For most people, this meant being baptized as an infant and being a member of the Church of England, even apart from any experience of conversion.

This kind of nominalism existed in Dissenting churches as well. Some churches, like the one in Newmarket, held to the practice of church membership, but it had largely lost its meaning. "Take our churches at large—there is no lack of names, but there is a lack of life. Else, how is it that our prayer meetings are so badly attended?"[6] Even as churches continued grow in membership, this made little difference in the lives of new members. Many people joining Spurgeon's church shared that the membership process from their previous church was quite meaningless, "I never saw the minister, I wrote a note to the Church, and they took me in."[7]

With church membership losing its meaning, some wondered if it even mattered at all. Increasingly, churches sought to attract people by watering down any lines of distinction. In a Christianized nation like England, it was easy for churches to reflect the tastes and values of the society. Spurgeon echoed the sentiment of many pastors in his day,

> They say, "Do not let us draw any hard and fast
> lines. A great many good people attend our

---

[5] *NPSP* 2:113–14.
[6] *NPSP* 2:113–14.
[7] *NPSP* 4:35.

services who may not be quite decided, but still their opinion should be consulted, and their vote should be taken upon the choice of a minister, and there should be entertainments and amusements, in which they can assist."[8]

For the sake of attraction, these pastors were willing for the lost to have a say in how worship services should be ordered and even in the calling of a new minister. But this strategy would ultimately backfire. Spurgeon believed making the church more like the world would result, not in the world coming over to the church, but the church going over to the world.

Regenerate Church Membership

These errors displayed a wrong understanding of the church. Spurgeon believed that the church was not made up of its leaders or the denominational structure, but of its people. And according to the New Testament, members of a local church, should be true disciples of Christ. Spurgeon gives this definition of a local church: "Any company of Christian men, gathered together in holy bonds of communion for the purpose of receiving God's ordinances, and preaching what they regard to be God's truths, is a church."[9] In another sermon, Spurgeon makes clear that by "Christian men," he means those, "who are believers in the Lord Jesus, men in whom the Holy Spirit has created faith in Christ, and the new nature of which faith is the sure index."[10]

Simply put, a local church is a congregation of born-again men and women, who gather under the preaching of the Word and observe Christ's ordinances. For churches to miss this fundamental

---

[8] *MTP* 33:212.
[9] *NPSP* 4:210.
[10] *MTP* 33:205.

truth would compromise their very existence. Churches get it wrong "when they admit into their membership persons who do not even profess to be converted. . . . An unholy, unregenerated church can never be the pillar of the truth."[11]

It was this conviction about the regenerate character of the church that shaped Spurgeon's membership practice. Each Sunday, countless visitors attended the services at the Metropolitan Tabernacle. How could Spurgeon know who was a true believer? How could he distinguish between a casual visitor and a true Christian? This is why church membership existed. God's sovereign and eternal purpose calls sinners to salvation. But along with that, God calls for Christians to "actually gather into the church." Therefore, it was the responsibility of churches to provide "a hedging and fencing about this church," which made it distinct from the world. This is what Spurgeon sought to implement in church membership.[12]

Church Membership and the Ordinances

Most fundamentally, church membership at the Tabernacle was made up of those who were baptized and were regularly allowed to take the Lord's Supper. Baptism was the initiatory ordinance by which a Christian publicly professed faith in Christ and was joined to the church. Because of the connection between baptism and membership, Spurgeon would not allow an unbaptized believer to join the church, including those who claimed to have been baptized as infants. Even though he valued his paedobaptist brothers and sisters, their differing views on baptism meant that they could not join

---

[11] *MTP* 24:552.

[12] "Touching all the members of this select assembly there is an eternal purpose which is the original reason of their being called, and to each of them there is an effectual calling whereby they actually gather into the church; then, also, there is a hedging and fencing about this church, by which it is maintained as a separate body, distinct from all the rest of mankind." *MTP* 24:542.

the church. Similarly, everyone who was baptized at the Tabernacle was brought into the membership of the church.

The Lord's Supper, then, was the ongoing ordinance of the church, which gave visible expression to their fellowship with one another. This was evident in the language of the Tabernacle minute books. When someone joined the church, they were brought "into full communion" with the church. An individual could not become a member until they participated in the Lord's Supper with the congregation. There was no such thing as a non-communing member. If a member was removed for non-attendance, the books recorded that he "neglected to fill up his place at the Lord's Table." If a person was removed from membership as an act of church discipline, they were no longer permitted to the Table. As the church carefully guarded the ordinances of the church, this also promoted a right understanding of church membership.

On one occasion, William Elvin was converted under the preaching of the gospel. As he met with the elders of the church, he gave solid evidence of his conversion, went through the membership process, and was eventually voted into membership and baptized. There was just one problem. He served with the Coldstream Guards and would soon be deployed to Ireland before he had the chance to take the Lord's Supper with the church. Would Spurgeon send Elvin off without bringing him into membership? Or would he bring Elvin in without having him partake of the Table? No. The minute books record, "after the public service, the pastor, elders, and deacons, brake bread with him & three godly men of the regiment in token of the fellowship of the whole church with our Brother and in the hope that in that regiment the Lord Jesus may lift up a standard." That occasion was a tangible reminder to this new Christian that he belonged to the body of Christ.

Countering Objections

As in our day, Christians in the nineteenth century had their objections to church membership. In his sermon, "Joining the Church," preached in 1869, Spurgeon concludes by responding to the typical arguments of his day.

> **"I can be a Christian without [church membership]."**
>
> Now, are you quite clear about that? You can be as good a Christian by disobedience to your Lord's commands as by being obedient? Well, suppose everybody else did the same, suppose all Christians in the world said, "I shall not join the Church." Why there would be no visible Church, there would be no ordinances. That would be a very bad thing, and yet, one doing it—what is right for one is right for all—why should not all of us do it? Then you believe that if you were to do an act which has a tendency to destroy the visible Church of God, you would be as good a Christian as if you did your best to build up that Church? I do not believe it, sir! nor do you either.
>
> You have not any such a belief; it is only a trumpery excuse for something else. There is a brick— a very good one. What is the brick made for? To help to build a house with. It is of no use for that brick to tell you that it is just as good a brick while it is kicking about on the ground as it would be in the house. It is a good-for-nothing brick; until it is built into the wall, it is no good. So you rolling-stone Christians, I do not believe that you are answering your purpose; you are living contrary to

the life which Christ would have you live, and you are much to blame for the injury you do.

"If I were to join the Church, I should feel it such a bond [i.e., heavy commitment] upon me."

Just what you ought to feel. Ought you not to feel that you are bound to holiness now, and bound to Christ now? Oh! those blessed bonds! If there is anything that could make me feel more bound to holiness than I am, I should like to feel that fetter, for it is only liberty to feel bound to godliness, and uprightness, and carefulness of living.

"If I were to join the Church, I am afraid that I should not be able to hold on."

You expect to hold on, I suppose, out of the Church—that is to say, you feel safer in disobeying Christ than in obeying him! Strange feeling that! Oh! you had better come and say, "My Master, I know thy saints ought to be united together in church-fellowship, for churches were instituted by thine apostles: and I trust I have grace to carry out the obligation: I have no strength of my own my Master, but my strength lies in resting upon thee: I will follow where thou leadest, and leave the rest to thee."

"I cannot join the Church; it is so imperfect . . .
I see so much that is wrong about Christians."

You, then, are perfect, of course! If so, I advise you
to go to heaven, and join the Church there, for
certainly you are not fit to join it on earth, and
would be quite out of place. . . . There is nothing
wrong in yourself, I suppose! I can only say, my
brethren, that if the Church of God is not better
than I am, I am sorry for it. I felt, when I joined the
Church, that I should be getting a deal more good
than I should be likely to bring into it, and with all
the faults I have seen in living these twenty years
or more in the Christian Church, I can say, as
an honest man, that the members of the Church
are the excellent of the earth, in whom is all my
delight, though they are not perfect, but a long
way from it. If, out of heaven, there are to be found
any who really live near to God, it is the members
of the Church of Christ.

"Ah . . . but there are a rare lot of hypocrites
[in the church]."

You are very sound and sincere yourself, I suppose?
I trust you are so, but then you ought to come and
join the Church, to add to its soundness by your
own. I am sure, my dear friends, none of you will
shut up your shops tomorrow morning, or refuse
to take a sovereign when a customer comes in,
because there happen to be some smashers about
who are dealing with bad coins.

No, not you, and you do not believe the theory of some, that because some professing Christians are hypocrites, therefore all are, for that would be as though you should say that, because some sovereigns are bad, therefore all are bad, which would be clearly wrong, for if all sovereigns were counterfeits, it would never pay for the counterfeiter to try to pass his counterfeits; it is just the quantity of good metal that passes off the bad.

There is a fine good quantity of respectable golden Christians still in the world and still in the Church, rest assured of that.

"I do not think . . . that I can join the Church; you see, it is so looked down upon."

Oh! what a blessed look-down that is! I do think, brethren, there is no honor in the world equal to that of being looked down upon by that which is called "Society" in this country. The most of people are slaves to what they call "respectability." Respectability! When a man puts on a coat on Sunday that he has paid for, when he worships God by night or by day, whether men see him or not: when he is an honest, straightforward man—I do not care how small his earnings are, he is a respectable man, and he need never bend his neck to the idea of Society or its artificial respectability! . . .

There is nothing better than the service of Christ. For my own part, to be despised, pointed at, hooted in the streets, called by all manner of ill-names—I would accept it all sooner than all the

stars of knighthoods and peerages, if the service
of Christ necessitated it, for this is the true honor
of the Christian when he truly serves his Master.[13]

Church membership is not optional because the church is not
optional. Church membership makes the distinction between the
church and the world visible. That distinction will be fully revealed
at the Last Day when Christ returns. But in this age, the church
exists as a warning to the world and a comfort to God's people that
Christ knows those who are His.

Spurgeon's Church Membership Practice

The membership numbers associated with Spurgeon's pastorate
in London are astonishing. When he first preached at the New Park
Street Chapel in December of 1853, the membership of the church
was likely under three hundred, though only a few dozen were in
attendance. Over the next thirty-eight years, Spurgeon took in
13,797 people into membership. Of that number 10,063 (73%) were
taken into membership through baptism, 2,764 (20%) through a
letter of transfer from another church, and 944 (7%) by profession.
On average, the church brought in about 400 people into membership each year. Of course, in a transient city like London, people
were constantly on the move. Some years, the church took in hundreds of new members and still saw a net decrease in membership.
Nonetheless, by the end of Spurgeon's ministry, the membership of
the Metropolitan Tabernacle was at 5,313 members.

Membership Transfers and Professions

A significant number of those who joined the Metropolitan
Tabernacle came from other Baptist churches. These people often

---

[13] *MTP* 60:295–97.

brought a letter of transfer from their previous church. The standard practice in those days among Baptist churches in the same association was simply to accept membership transfers from one another because they all shared the same theological and ecclesiological convictions. Spurgeon, however, understood that despite any doctrinal agreement, their practice of church membership could vary hugely.[14] Given the lax discipline in so many churches, Spurgeon would not take transfers into membership automatically. He still required a pastoral interview with an elder, followed by a congregational vote.

Some applicants were admitted "by profession," meaning that they had already been baptized but did not have a letter of transfer from another church. Many reasons could exist for this. Perhaps their previous church baptized them without taking them into membership (a practice Spurgeon considered disorderly). Or perhaps they came from a church that refused to grant a letter of dismission. For example, many strict communion Baptist churches did not grant letters to members who wanted to join the Tabernacle because of their open communion position. All these applicants "by profession" underwent the full membership process.

---

[14] "In dealing with such as are members of other churches, we have been by sad experience compelled to exercise more caution than at first seemed needful. The plan we adopt is to have the person seen by an elder, who enters particulars in the transfer book. If there appears to be any difficulty, an interview is arranged with one of the pastors, who investigates the case on its own merits, as alas! he has discovered that membership with some churches is not always a guarantee even of morality. Some churches retain a name upon their books for years after the person has ceased to commune; and frequently when he has passed away from all knowledge of or connection with the church, it will nevertheless grant a transfer as if all were satisfactory. We record this with mingled shame and sorrow." *S&T* 1869:54.

Conversions in the Church

Spurgeon was glad to have additions by transfers or by profession, but he would have found it shameful if such people made up most of the congregation. Above all, he wanted to see people brought into the church from the world.[15]

The vast majority (more than 70%) of those who joined the Metropolitan Tabernacle were received by baptism. This meant that most of the membership of the Tabernacle was made up of those who were converted through the ministry of the church. He found these new converts to be some of the best members of the church, bringing fresh zeal and warmth to the rest of the congregation.

Spurgeon did not adopt the revivalist practices of his day. Churches often held revival meetings and would publish the results, "Last night, fourteen souls were under conviction, fifteen were justified, and eight received full sanctification." Seeing these kinds of reports, Spurgeon groaned, "I am weary of this public bragging, this counting of unhatched chickens, this exhibition of doubtful spoils."[16] Instead of manipulating people to make "decisions" for Christ, Spurgeon encouraged inquirers to meet with a pastor or an elder so that they might be able to talk about the gospel. Those who professed faith in Christ were not counted but encouraged toward baptism and membership in the church. He counseled pastors to follow his example.[17]

---

[15] "I should reckon it to be a burning disgrace if it could be said, 'The large church under that man's pastoral care is composed of members whom he has stolen away from other Christian churches.' No, but I value beyond all price the godless, the careless, who are brought out from the world into communion with Christ." *MTP* 15:90.

[16] Charles H. Spurgeon, *The Soul-Winner, or How to Lead Sinners to the Savior* (Pasadena, TX: Pilgrim Publications, 2007), 15.

[17] "After each sermon, announce that inquirers will be immediately seen, and encourage them to stay behind. Also publish frequently the way of joining the church, and urge secret believers to confess their Lord. Let no one say, 'I wish to

For those who professed to be converted under Spurgeon's ministry, the only counting of converts on Spurgeon's part was in the membership reports of the church, published once a year at the church's annual meeting.

The Membership Process for New Converts

Spurgeon did not think it possible to have a perfect church here on earth. Nonetheless, he was committed to the principle of regenerate church membership. Rather than promoting "doubtful spoils," Spurgeon implemented a membership process that gave careful examination to each applicant and involved the entire church in the process.

There were at least six steps in joining the church.[18]

---

be baptized, but do not; know where to apply.' Keep the church agencies above board, and make plain paths for the feet of seekers." *S&T* 1872:440.

[18] Writing in 1869, Spurgeon's brother and associate pastor, James, describes the membership process at the Metropolitan Tabernacle: "All persons anxious to join our church are requested to apply personally upon any Wednesday evening, between six and nine o'clock, to the elders, two or more of whom attend in rotation every week for the purpose of seeing inquirers. When satisfied, the case is entered by the elder in one of a set of books provided for the purpose, and a card is given bearing a corresponding number to the page of the book in which particulars of the candidate's experience are recorded. Once a month, or oftener when required, the junior pastor appoints a day to see the persons thus approved of by the elders. If the pastor is satisfied, he nominates an elder or church member as visitor, and at the next church meeting asks the church to send him to enquire as to the moral character and repute of the candidate. If the visitor be satisfied he requests the candidate to attend with him at the following or next convenient church meeting, to come before the church and reply to such questions as may be put from the chair, mainly with a view to elicit expressions of his trust in the Lord Jesus, and hope of salvation through his blood, and any such facts of his spiritual history as may convince the church of the genuineness of the case. . . . After the statement before the church, the candidate withdraws, the visitor gives in his report, and the vote of the church is taken; when the candidate has professed his faith by immersion, which is administered by the junior pastor after a week-day service, he is received by the pastor at the first monthly communion, when the right hand of fellowship is given to him in the name of the church, and his name is entered on the roll of members." *S&T* 1869:53–54.

1. An elder interview: A visitor would come on a weekday to meet with an elder of the church to share their testimony and understanding of the gospel. The elder would ask follow-up questions and record the testimony in one of the church's Testimony Books. If the elder felt this was a sincere profession of faith, they would be recommended to meet with the Pastor.

2. Pastoral interview: Spurgeon would review the testimonies that were recorded, and, on another day, the candidate would come to meet with him. Some interviews showed a clear conversion, and Spurgeon had the joy of rejoicing in God's grace with the candidate. Other cases resulted in further questions to the applicant, as Spurgeon examined their story and understanding of the gospel. In either case, Spurgeon was glad that the interview process involved multiple officers of the church and was not the sole decision of one person.

3. Proposal to the congregation and the assignment of a visitor: The next step would be for the elder who performed the interview to present the name of the applicant and propose him for membership at a congregational meeting of the church. The congregation would then vote to appoint a visitor to make an inquiry.

4. Visitor inquiry: The appointed visitor, usually a deacon or an elder, would go to the candidate's place of work, home, or neighborhood and ask about his character and reputation. What were they like at home? Did they have a good reputation? Was there any evidence of a changed life? On one occasion, a policeman applied for membership at the Tabernacle, and Spurgeon encouraged the visitor to make a careful inquiry at the police station as to his character and reputation. These inquiries not only verified the candidate's profession of faith, but also had the effect of making that profession public in their communities, opening doors for the gospel.

5. Congregational interview and vote: Once the messenger finished his inquiry, he would report his findings at the next congregational meeting. The candidate would be present at this meeting. He would be introduced to the congregation via a brief interview from the chair. Then, he would be dismissed, and the congregation would vote on his membership.

6. *Baptism and communion:* Finally, the candidate would be scheduled for baptism, if necessary, and after the baptism, at the next communion service, he would receive the right hand of fellowship before the congregation and officially become a member of the church.

Some criticized the Tabernacle's rigorous membership process. It was not Spurgeon's intention to make the process needlessly difficult or long. Some Baptist churches were so strict in their practice of membership that they lost sight of the miracle and joy of conversion.

> [In these churches] You must be summered and wintered, and tried this way and that, before you can be received; and when you are received, the members are sure to rub their hands together, and say, "Well, it's a serious thing to receive members;" and they are about as glad as I suppose a poor man might be, who had nineteen children, when there is another coming to eat of the scanty loaf. They seem to think that the addition of so many new members would make the whole of the old members so much the poorer.[19]

Other applicants were eager to show off their knowledge of the Bible and theology, thinking that these things would commend them to church membership.[20] But this was not Spurgeon's approach.

---

[19] *MTP* 53:460.

[20] "Suppose now a person getting up in the church meeting . . . and saying, 'Brethren, I come to unite with you. I know the Greek Testament; I have also

For all the rigor of the membership process at the Tabernacle, it existed to test something very simple: the credibility of one's profession of faith in Christ.

As such, the membership process served to filter out those of nominal faith. James Spurgeon wrote, "We have never yet found it tend to keep members out of our midst, while we have known it of service in detecting a mistake or satisfying a doubt previously entertained. We deny that it keeps away any worth having."[21] Those who patiently went through the process demonstrated greater sincerity in their profession of faith and commitment to the church. For the 13,797 individuals who joined the church during Spurgeon's day, they were all serious about their commitment to the church.

Conducting Membership Interviews

It was never Spurgeon's intention for meetings with an elder or pastor to be intimidating. He saw each membership interview as a chance to begin shepherding the individual. Those who were genuinely converted would have the joy of sharing their story. For those who struggled to explain the gospel or gave insufficient evidence of conversion, the church gained an opportunity to begin walking alongside them and help them grow in their understanding of

---

read a good deal in Latin; I understand the Vulgate; I can now, if you please, give you the 1st chapter of Mark in Greek, or the 2nd chapter of Exodus in Hebrew, if you like. I have also, from my youth up, given myself to the study of the natural and applied sciences. I think I am master of rhetoric, and I am able to reason logically' . . . I am sure, dear friends, if a man were to say all that, before I put it to the vote whether he should be admitted to church-membership, I should say, 'This dear brother has not any idea of what he came here for. He came here to make a confession that he was a living man in Christ Jesus, and he has been only trying to prove to us that he is a learned man. That is not what we want;' . . . we only ask you, if you wish to join the church, to be able to confess that you are a changed character, that you are a new man, that you are willing to be obedient to Christ and to his ordinances, and then we are only too glad to receive you into our midst." *MTP* 51:477.

[21] *S&T* 1869:53–54.

the gospel, perhaps for the very first time. Whatever their spiritual maturity, Spurgeon's assurance to the fearful applicant was this: "Be sure of this, if you have really believed in Jesus, you shall not find the church terrible to you."[22]

In Bunyan's *Pilgrim's Progress*, Spurgeon sees Christian's arrival at the House Beautiful as his entrance into the church. There, Christian encounters chained lions at the entrance along with the porter of the house, who urges him to enter. In both these images, Spurgeon sees the work of pastors and church officers to receive people into the church. On one hand, the officers are the lions of the church, put in place to guard the church. But they are chained "by the intense love they bear both to their Lord and to all pilgrims to Zion."[23] The pastor is the porter who calls pilgrims to join the church and examines their profession of faith as they enter.

In his commentary on *Pilgrim's Progress*, Spurgeon offers the following advice for pastors and church elders as they conduct membership interviews:

1. *Balance both grace and wisdom in the interview:* The officer of the church, who is appointed to see candidates for membership, should be "grave" in his carriage and "beautiful" in his character; he should be discreet, yet affectionate; desirous neither to be deceived

---

[22] "Whenever I hear of candidates being alarmed at coming before our elders, or seeing the pastor, or making confession of faith before the church, I wish I could say to them: 'Dismiss your fears, beloved ones; we shall be glad to see you, and you will find your intercourse with us a pleasure rather than a trial.' So far from wishing to repel you, if you really do love the Savior, we shall be glad enough to welcome you. If we cannot see in you the evidence of a great change, we shall kindly point out to you our fears, and shall be thrice happy to point you to the Savior; but be sure of this, if you have really believed in Jesus, you shall not find the church terrible to you." *MTP* 17:198–99.

[23] *MTP* 37:77.

nor to let his fellow-members be deceived; anxious not to be too severe, so as to keep out of the church those who are truly the Lord's; and, on the other hand, not to be too lax, so as to receive those who are not His people.

2. *Examine the applicant's understanding of their sin:* That question was put in order to ascertain whether he knew what he was by nature; for, if you do not know what you are by nature, you do not really begin to know anything aright. If you have never discovered that you were born in sin, and shapen in iniquity,—if you have never realized that you are a sinner, lost and undone . . . you are not fit to be entertained at the Palace Beautiful, for you evidently are not a true Christian.

3. *Examine the applicant's assurance of their salvation:* . . . and, further, if you have never lost your burden at the cross,—you are not fit to be entertained at the Palace Beautiful, for you evidently are not a true Christian. I am afraid that there are many people who do not know whither they are going,—whether to Heaven or to hell,—though they have a faint hope that, possibly, all may be well with them at the last. There are also some who assert that a man cannot know whether he is saved till he gets into another world. Surely, they must have read a different Bible from the one I read every day; for that seems to me to speak very clearly upon this matter: . . . "Therefore being justified by faith, we have peace with

God through our Lord Jesus Christ." Surely, a man is not saved without knowing it; and he does not possess peace with God without being aware that he has that peace.

4. *Ask for the applicant's testimony of conversion:* We shall say to you, "You profess to be on the road to Heaven; but how did you commence to walk in that way? What led you to go on pilgrimage? How came you to realize your need of a Savior? How did the work of grace begin in your heart?" We shall not want you to tell us the day and the hour when you were converted. Some of us could tell that about ourselves, but others could not; and there will be no [pastor] who will be angry with you if you cannot.

5. *Ask about the change that has taken place since conversion:* We shall want to know what your experience has been since you became a Christian,—whether you have proved the power of the prayer, because God has answered your petitions,—whether, when you have been tempted, you have been able to resist the tempter, and overcome him. We shall also ask you what you are doing for Christ, and what you think of Christ, and what are your habits with regard to reading Scriptures, and private prayer, and such things.[24]

---

[24] C. H. Spurgeon, *Pictures from Pilgrim's Progress* (Pasadena, TX: Pilgrim Publications, 1992), 124–27.

Following Christian's interview with Discretion, three members of the church are brought in to talk with him—Prudence, Piety, and Charity. Spurgeon understood these to be the visitors making an inquiry for the church: "Prudence, who does not want to let any hypocrites in; Piety, who understands spiritual matters, and knows how to search the heart; and Charity, who judges kindly, yet justly, according to the love of Christ which is shed abroad in her heart." For Spurgeon, prudence, piety, and charity were to be qualities not only of the pastor, but for all involved in the membership process.

Conclusion

Did Spurgeon ever take shortcuts in his membership interviews? Did his practice ever adjust over time? Preaching in 1884, Spurgeon declared,

> Oh, brothers, on that day on which I lately saw forty persons one by one, and listened to their experience and proposed them to the church, I felt as weary as ever a man did in reaping the heaviest harvest. I did not merely give them a few words as enquirers, but examined them as candidates with my best judgment.

Thirty-two years into his pastoral ministry, even after having taken thousands of people into membership, Spurgeon still believed that one of his primary responsibilities as a pastor was to examine those coming into the church for membership one-by-one.

Today, as in Spurgeon's day, church membership continues to be overlooked. Church growth experts encourage pastors to promote a mindset of "belonging before believing." Visitors and attenders are to be included in virtually every part of the life of the church, even prior to professing faith and committing to the church. In these churches, the membership process becomes more logistical than pastoral, much less spiritually meaningful. In this way, the distinction between the church and the world is lowered, and the membership of the church is marked more by the world than by the gospel.

Against such trends, Spurgeon reminds us that church membership matters because it preserves what a church is: a congregation of believers. Certainly, practicing regenerate church membership will be difficult. It was for Spurgeon. After conducting forty membership interviews in one day, he said, "I thought that if I had many days of that sort I must die, but I also wished it might be my lot to die in that fashion. Having so many coming to confess Christ my mind was crushed beneath the weight of blessing, but I would gladly be overwhelmed again."[25] Yes, regenerate church membership is hard work but Spurgeon reminds us that it is well worth it, for our joy and for the health of the church.

---

[25] *MTP* 30:310.

5

WATCHING OVER THE CHURCH

MEANINGFUL CHURCH MEMBERSHIP

"I'll Kill Old Roads, that I Will!"

Spurgeon was probably five or six when he first participated in church discipline. Growing up in the home of his grandfather James, pastor in Stambourne, Spurgeon got to see the inner workings of the church. He watched his grandfather prepare and pray over his sermons. He attended all the meetings of the church. He accompanied him to tea with the local vicar to discuss how their congregations could cooperate. He also saw the heartache of pastoral ministry.

On one occasion, Spurgeon saw the sorrow that a member of the church, Thomas Roads, brought on his grandfather with his drinking. Despite the godly pastor's appeals, Roads continued to frequent the local pub and fall into drunkenness. Finally, young Spurgeon had enough and declared, "I'll kill old Roads, that I will!" His grandfather tried to calm him down, but Spurgeon stormed out of the house. James didn't know what to make of that, but before long, Roads called on him, ready to confess and repent. Of course, James was ready to forgive, but he asked what brought about the change of heart. Roads answered,

"I was a-sitting in the public just having my pipe and mug of beer, when that child comes in,—to think an old man like me should be took to task, and reproved by a bit of a child like that! Well, he points at me with his finger, just so, and says, 'What doest thou here, Elijah? sitting with the ungodly; and you a member of a church, and breaking your pastor's heart. I'm ashamed of you! I wouldn't break my pastor's heart, I'm sure.' And then he walks away. Well, I did feel angry; but I knew it was all true, and I was guilty; so I put down my pipe, and did not touch my beer, but hurried away to a lonely spot, and cast myself down before the Lord, confessing my sin and begging for forgiveness."[1]

Okay, so maybe this wasn't a formal process of church discipline. But even at a young age, Spurgeon understood that church membership meant something and was moved by the love of a pastor for his wayward sheep. Years later, he would himself become a pastor and experience the heartache of ministry.

When Spurgeon became the pastor at Waterbeach, people loved his sermons. But he was not content with the praise of his church members. "I could never be satisfied with a full congregation, and the kind expressions of friends; I longed to hear that hearts had been broken, that tears had been seen streaming from the eyes of penitents." He wanted to know that someone was *converted* under his preaching. He wondered, "The gospel has saved me, but then somebody else preached it; will it save anybody else now that I preach it?"

When he first heard the news that someone had been converted under his preaching, he was overjoyed. He felt "like a diver

---

[1] *Autobiography* 1:24.

who has been down to the depths of the sea, and brought up a rare pearl." His joy was even greater given the dramatic nature of this conversion. Thomas Charles was the terror of the neighborhood, who "could drink more than any man for miles around, a man who would curse and swear, and never knew a thought of fear." Yet for some reason, he was drawn to young Spurgeon. He began attending the services at Waterbeach, and after several weeks, Mr. Charles professed repentance. His life was remarkably changed. "He gave up his drinking and swearing, and was in many respects an exemplary individual. All the parish was astonished." Eventually, Mr. Charles was baptized and joined the church, and Spurgeon "set him down as being a bright jewel in the Redeemer's crown."

At first, Mr. Charles was one of the most zealous members of the church. If there was any work to be done in the church, he would do it. But tragically, this would not last. As the months passed, he began to waver.

> He began to think he had been a little too fanatical, a little too earnest. He slunk up to the place of worship instead of coming boldly in; he gradually forsook the week-night service, and then neglected the Sabbath-day; and, though often warned, and often rebuked, he returned to his old habits, and any thoughts of God or godliness that he had ever known, seemed to die away.[2]

Despite repeated warnings and rebukes, Mr. Charles returned to his old life. The church member who was a living testimony to the power of God was now once again found drunk in the streets, much to the shame of the church. Mr. Charles eventually "became worse than he was before" and never turned back to the faith. Through

---

[2] *Autobiography* 1:238.

"many bitter tears," Spurgeon eventually had no choice but to lead his church to excommunicate his first convert.[3]

The story of Mr. Charles reminded Spurgeon that the road to heaven was narrow and many would not persevere to the end. As much as he longed to celebrate his first convert, he could not jeopardize the purity of the church. Spurgeon would go on to see many more men and women profess repentance and faith under his preaching, but a profession of faith was only the beginning. As a pastor, Spurgeon understood that his responsibility was not only to bring them into the church, but to help them make it safely to heaven and call any who wandered to come back to the truth.

Last chapter, we considered how Spurgeon brought people into the membership of the church. In this chapter, we'll look at how Spurgeon cared for and kept track of his people once they were members of the church. In other words, how did he make membership at the Tabernacle meaningful?

The Challenge of Meaningful Membership

Throughout the nineteenth century, the city of London saw remarkable growth. In 1801, the population of greater London was just over 1 million. By the time the Metropolitan Tabernacle was constructed in 1861, population had more than tripled to 3.2 million. By Spurgeon's death in 1892, that number had increased to 5.6 million. These communities, however, weren't static. People weren't only moving to London; people were moving inside London and leaving London as well. Unsanitary conditions, overcrowding, poor housing, pollution, economic depression, and many other factors prompted people to look for better opportunities in other

---

[3] For the story of Mr. Charles, see *Autobiography* 1:238–239 and *LS* 1:339–41.

parts of the city, the country, and throughout the English-speaking world.

All of this made pastoring in London difficult. How could pastors maintain a meaningful and accurate membership amid all the transiency? Spurgeon was not content to focus on large numbers in the church. He sought to have a membership where each member was known by the elders, accounted for, and actively engaged in the life of the church. This was not only a pastoral commitment. It was a theological conviction. He wanted to pastor a *real* church.

> I would urge upon the resolve to have no church unless it be a real one. The fact is, that too frequently religious statistics are shockingly false . . . Let us not keep names on our books when they are only names. Certain of the good old people like to keep them there, and cannot bear to have them removed; but when you do not know where the individuals are, nor what they are, how can you count them? They are gone to America, or Australia, or to heaven, but as far as your roll is concerned they are with you still. Is this a right thing? It may not be possible to be absolutely accurate, but let us aim at it. . . . Keep your church real and effective, or make no report. A merely nominal church is a lie. Let it be what it professes to be.[4]

For Spurgeon, the church was not a building or a report, but a people. And the membership roll declared to the world who her members were. It was not a sentimental record of all those who were at one point involved with the church. Rather, it was an expression

---

[4] *GFW* 41–42.

of the ongoing accountability and commitment among the church members.

Churches in his day were quite happy to report inflated statistics, but Spurgeon believed that such practices compromised the truthfulness of the church, making it a church in name only. As difficult as it was, Spurgeon wanted to pastor a real church. Therefore, along with the elders, he worked tirelessly to know and keep up with his members, not only vetting those who entered but also pursuing those who strayed and removing any who left.

The Hard Work of Meaningful Membership

Over the thirty-eight years of Spurgeon's ministry at the Tabernacle, 9,281 people were removed from membership, which was 67 percent of those who were brought into membership. In other words, for every three members that the church took into membership, two of them would go through the removal process. With nearly 14,000 joining the Metropolitan Tabernacle over his ministry, perhaps what should impress us is not that the membership was more than 5,000, but that it was less than 10,000!

Each removal took place in a congregational meeting as members heard about deaths in the congregation and received letters from other churches requesting a transfer and from members asking to resign their membership. In each case, except for deaths, the congregation voted to approve each removal.[5] Maintaining an accurate membership was more than just a logistical matter. Spurgeon used these removals as teaching opportunities, giving members a deeper perspective of the work in the church.

---

[5] "On receipt of application from any church for a transfer, the letter is read to the church, with the detailed account from our books, giving a brief but complete history of the case, when and how received, the attendance of the person while a member with us, and reasons for seeking removal. The church is then advised to authorize the usual letter of dismission to be sent." S&T 1869:54–55.

Naturally, many of the losses were due to death. At times, these deaths included active, long-standing, beloved members of the church. On one occasion, Spurgeon lost two vital deacons in the span of nine days. Such losses were felt deeply by the church, and people wondered how the ministries of the church would continue. Though grieved by these deaths, Spurgeon saw them as a call for those who remained to redouble their efforts.

> Brethren, let us take a blessed revenge on death; and if he takes from our numbers, let us, as God helps us, increase the real efficiency of the church, by each of us endeavoring to become double what we formerly were in the service of our Master . . . if some of the troops have fought the good fight, and exchanged the sword and shield for the palm-branch and the harp, let us who are left pray with all our might unto the Lord God of hosts to strengthen us in this day of battle, that we may not go till we have finished our part of the fight.[6]

For those who moved away from the area, Spurgeon urged them to quickly find and join another evangelical church. Many members left London and moved to other parts of England, or even farther. Many of these members undoubtedly felt a deep love for the Tabernacle. They could keep up with the church through weekly printed sermons and *The Sword and the Trowel*. Because of this, they might drag their heels in joining another church. But Spurgeon did not want them to "linger out a merely nominal connection with us." He urged them to join a church where they could serve. To nudge these departed members, they were given expiring

---

[6] *MTP* 39:4.

membership certificates.[7] Barring unusual circumstances, the church did not keep members living out of the area on the membership roll indefinitely. They anticipated that these departed members would either join another church, or their membership would eventually lapse. Most of them, however, did find another church, and the Tabernacle was happy to grant a letter of dismission.

One exception to all this appears to be in the case of emigration. Because international communication was expensive and slow, those who emigrated to another country were granted expiring membership certificates and removed from membership automatically. Spurgeon was especially glad for those who went to lands where Christianity was not yet established. From the frontiers of the American West to Australia, Canada, and other parts of the British Empire, the Metropolitan Tabernacle sent hundreds of its members all over the world.

> For my part, I thank God for the many whom we
> lose by emigration. I am glad that some friends
> have gone to America. . . . Look still further away
> to Australia, so largely peopled by those who are
> of our race. What a mercy that it is so! Would
> you have those lands given up to Romanism, or
> to Mohammedanism, or to Paganism? God forbid!
> Salt ought not to be kept in a box; it is meant to be
> rubbed into the meat, and Christians are intended
> to be scattered all over the carcass of this world,

---

[7] "When, in the order of God's providence, any of our number are removed from us, and are not able to attend, a certificate is given for three, six, or twelve months, which must then be renewed, and a report of the reason for renewal given, or the membership will lapse, unless in special cases. We much prefer commending our brethren to the fellowship of other churches, where they may be of service, than to have them linger out a merely nominal connection with us. We have thus sent from us 166 in the course of last year, we hope to the strengthening of the churches and the spread of the truth." S&T 1869:54.

to salt it all, and act with purifying and preserving power in every place.[8]

Though the church would never see them again, Spurgeon trusted that God would use these former members around the world.

Likewise, the church rejoiced to hear about former members serving and strengthening other churches. In many cases, members would join smaller churches, where they could take what they learned at the Tabernacle and use it to be a blessing to those congregations. Spurgeon observed that a faithful member at his church might never become a deacon or elder, but in a smaller church, he could easily step into leadership. As he preached around the country, he would often run into former members who now served in leadership in their churches.[9] Throughout his ministry, Spurgeon saw thousands of members removed to join other churches. It is impossible to calculate the impact that these removals had on other churches in England.

That's not to say that members of the Tabernacle didn't miss their departed brothers and sisters. Spurgeon felt each loss as the pastor. Speaking of members who left, he declared, "I feel this as bereavement; I cannot bear to miss the face of a single one from the members of the church. There is a sort of sacred bond of union that binds all together. . . . It is a sad thing to see them separated from

---

[8] *MTP* 46:435.

[9] "Often, the removal of a Christian out of a particular place is in order that he may be more helpful to another community than he is in his present position. I have frequently seen brethren, who were just ordinary members of this church, good, useful people, but they did not attain to any very great prominence; yet, in another place, they have been exceedingly useful. I go into the country to preach, and the deacon shakes hands with me, and as I look at him, I say, 'Ah! I recollect you.' 'Well, sir,' he replies, 'I moved away from London, some years ago, and the Lord has been pleased to put me here, so that I may help this little cause. It has been strengthened, I hope, by my coming;' and I find the brother greatly developed by being transplanted." *MTP* 46:434–35.

us, and that has happened to this church over and over again."[10] At the same time, Spurgeon refused to be territorial. He rejoiced to see other churches blessed by those who were converted and discipled under his ministry. Each time the congregation approved a removal, they were to do so with cheerfulness, knowing that the cause of Christ was served.

> If your brethren and sisters are gone where they can be more useful, God speed them! Freely and cheerfully let them go. A heart that should try to keep all the blood within itself would be no source of life to the body; nay, it could not itself live; but the heart that continually pumps in the blood and then pumps it out again, is the one that is serving its proper purpose. That is how churches should do; let them not be parsimonious, but rather prodigal in the cause of God.[11]

Dealing with Nonattendance

In the previous section, we dealt with deaths and membership resignations. But what if a member just stopped attending? In such a large congregation, how did the elders of the Metropolitan Tabernacle keep track of their people?

There were three main strategies. First, Spurgeon taught his people to care for one another. In a church of several thousand, it was impossible for the elders to keep track of every member perfectly. Instead, the members of the church were enlisted to help their pastors in caring for the church.[12] Spurgeon did not want the

---

[10] *MTP* 48:197–98.

[11] *MTP* 46:435.

[12] "Let the watching be done by all the members: by the officers of the church first, and then by every individual. . . . Guide them and cheer them on. Help their weakness, bear with their ignorance and impetuosity, and correct their mistakes.

Tabernacle to be a church where members could hide in the crowd and remain strangers. Rather, through formal means like Bible studies and service ministries, and informal means like friendships and intentional conversations, he hoped that all the members of the church would be connected in meaningful relationships. If someone stopped attending, it should not go unnoticed.

Second, Spurgeon organized the church into districts and assigned elders to oversee the members within their district. We don't know for sure how large these districts were. Given the church's size, even if the congregation were evenly divided among the elders, there could be as many as 200 members per elder. It's also not clear how proactive the elders were on a day-to-day basis in visiting the people in their district. The elder minutes reveal that some elders were more engaged in their pastoral work than others. Many members also lived too far away from London to be included in a district. Despite these limitations, Spurgeon believed that organizing the church into districts allowed for a division of labor among the elders. This helped them better care for the membership.

The main tool, however, for tracking non-attenders was the use of communion tickets. At least once a year, members would receive a membership card confirming their membership in good standing at the Tabernacle. Attached to that card would be numbered communion tickets. At each communion service, those tickets would admit a member to the table and indicate to the elders the attendance of that member. After each service, the communion tickets

---

I charge you, my beloved sisters, be nursing mothers in the church, and you, my brethren, be fathers to these young people, that they may be enabled by your help through God's Spirit to hold on their way. It is an evil thing to receive members, and never care for them afterwards. Among so many some must escape our supervision, but if all the members of the church were watchful this could not be; each would have some one to care for him, each one would have a friend to whom to tell his troubles and his cares. Watch over the church, then, I pray you." *MTP* 20:215–16.

were checked against the membership books and if any were absent from communion for more than three months, the elders were notified. The elder overseeing that member's district would then visit him, or the elders would send him a letter.

Sometimes an investigation would result in the bittersweet discovery that a member had "gone to heaven," and no one had notified the church. In other cases, the elders might discover that these members had joined other churches or moved away from the area. In these cases, the elders would proceed with the process of removing these people from membership.

In many cases, the inquiry would result in varying reasons for a member's non-attendance. When it came to these cases, Spurgeon refused to implement a hard and fast rule regarding how to deal with local members who were non-attending (i.e., after six months of non-attendance, remove them from membership). Each case was an opportunity for exercising pastoral care and wisdom.

> If a sheep has strayed let us seek it; to disown it in a hurry is not the Master's method. Ours is to be the labor and the care, for we are overseers of the flock of Christ to the end that all may be presented faultless before God. One month's absence from the house of God is, in some cases, a deadly sign of a profession renounced, while in others a long absence is an affliction to be sympathized with, and not a crime to be capitally punished.[13]

Reasons for non-attendance varied. Sometimes, it was as simple as forgotten communion tickets or they just happened to miss consecutive communion services. These members were encouraged to bring their tickets next time. Often, there were challenges

---

[13] S&T 1872:198.

that prevented members from attending the church. These cases required pastoral care, not rigid regulations. Some pastors believed that churches should automatically remove non-attenders after a period of time. Spurgeon, however, encouraged pastors to show patience toward non-attenders and shared the following stories from his own experience.

> For instance, a person reduced in circumstances, but quite unwilling to make his circumstances known, had pawned the garments in which he was wont to appear among us. The same spirit which led him to keep his wants private induced him also to worship among strangers while his raiment was shabby. I do not justify the spirit, neither dare I say a hard word against it, but a gentle rebuke and a brotherly gift soon enabled the afflicted friend to fill up his place to his own intense delight.
>
> In another instance, a member had gone to Australia and back upon a voyage as steward, and reappeared shortly after enquiry had been made; his exclusion would have greatly pained the mind of a most worthy brother, and would have been an outrage upon Christian love.
>
> A mother of many children had also been very ill herself for some considerable time, during which the family had removed, that she could not be found, then followed an interesting event which increased her cares, and not for some months could she again occupy her place among us. Her husband, an ungodly man, would not take the trouble to communicate her change of abode, and thus by the heartless rule suggested above she would have been excluded from the church;

our knowledge of her gracious character led us to wait, and she returned to worship and to the Lord's table at the first possible moment.

Many varieties of circumstances may thus render absence no sin; but surely only for sin, removal to another church, or utter failure to find out a brother's whereabouts after earnest searching, ought we to erase a name from the roll of our membership.[14]

Even while Spurgeon aimed to have a meaningful and accurate membership roll, he did not go about the task mechanically. Rather, it was a messy process that required patience, wisdom, and care. "The best plan is to deal with every case on its own merits, without regard either to rule or precedent, looking only to the great general principles of the Word of God, and asking the guidance of the Holy Spirit."[15]

The Painful Work of Church Discipline

There were some cases, however, where non-attendance served as "a deadly sign of a profession renounced." The elders pursued these cases pastorally. But on some occasions, if a member persisted in unrepentance, it resulted in church discipline. Church discipline, also known as excommunication, was the congregation's act to remove an unrepentant member from their membership. In removing a person from membership, the church no longer affirmed his profession of faith and therefore, he could no longer participate at the Lord's Table. Spurgeon saw the practice of church discipline clearly commanded by Christ and the apostles in passages like Matthew 18 and 1 Corinthians 5. Over the course of Spurgeon's

---

[14] *S&T* 1872:198.
[15] *S&T* 1872:198.

ministry, 253 members were excluded or excommunicated from the church.

Though the elders led in matters of church discipline, Spurgeon believed that only the congregation could take the final step of excommunicating a member. Therefore, it was important for his people to understand why church discipline mattered. Spurgeon regularly made church discipline a point of application in his preaching. To my knowledge, he never preached a sermon dedicated to church discipline. But it was woven into his teaching on the life and responsibility of the church. Rather than simply having the congregation rubber stamp the elders' decision, he wanted to make sure they understood what they were doing when it came to these weighty matters. So, what did Spurgeon teach about church discipline?

First, church discipline guarded the church from error. Sin and false teaching spread. Church discipline exposes sin and protects church members from it. Spurgeon reminded his people, "This is one of the benefits of Church discipline when we are enabled to carry it out under God, that it does nip error in the very bud, and thus those who as yet are not infected are kept from it by the blessed providence of God through the instrumentality of the Church."[16]

Church discipline also upholds the church's purity. The church is to be holy and distinct from the world. The membership process filtered out many of the nominal, but it wasn't a perfect system. If the church harbors members who are living in serious, unrepentant sin, then it fails to live out the holiness that is the necessary fruit of the gospel. For a church so large, it was a difficult task for the elders to know every instance of serious, unrepentant sin. But

---

[16] *MTP* 8:94.

Spurgeon urged the congregation to care for one another and to be willing to confront sin.[17]

Third, church discipline aims for the restoration of the sinner. While dealing with sin is never pleasant, Spurgeon reminded his people not to lose sight of the hope of discipline, namely the sinner's repentance. Reflecting on 1 Corinthians 5:5, Spurgeon writes,

> If a man hath fallen, and even if the church be obliged to put him away, we do not deliver such a one to Satan that he may blaspheme, but that he may learn not to blaspheme. The object of church discipline should always be the good of the person who has to endure it . . . beloved, seek the wandering sheep, remembering that there will be more joy in the presence of the angels of God over one restored wanderer than over ninety and nine that went not astray.[18]

During Spurgeon's ministry, the membership reports record twenty-one members who were excommunicated, but eventually repented of their sin and were joyfully restored to fellowship.

One example of this is William Catchpole. In 1857, he was disciplined before the church for the sin of adultery. But four years later, the minute books record the following motion,

> William Catchpole came before the Church and professed his deep and unfeigned repentance of

---

[17] "If we know that members are living in gross sin, and do not deal with them either by way of censure or excommunication, in accordance with the teaching of Christ and his apostles, we become accomplices in their sin. I often tremble about this matter, for it is no easy task where we count our members by thousands; but may we never wink at sin, either in ourselves or in others! May you all, beloved, exercise a jealous oversight over one another, and so help to keep one another right!" *MTP* 53:427.

[18] *MTP* 15:453.

the sin for which he was excommunicated and his hope that the Lord had restored to him the light of his countenance, and Brother Moore, having stated that he had thoroughly investigated the case and could with confidence recommend him, our Pastor also informing the Church that no persons had offered any objection and that the offended brother was willing that he should be received, it is therefore agreed that he be restored to membership with this Church.[19]

Catchpole's membership in the church was a reminder of the gracious fruit of church discipline to bring sinners back to repentance.

Finally, Spurgeon taught his people that church discipline expressed Christ's rule here on earth. Reflecting on Jesus's words from Matthew 18:18–19, Spurgeon sought to give his people a heavenly perspective of their church meetings, especially in matters of discipline and restoration.

This being done, according to Christ's rule— justly, impartially, lovingly, with prayer—that which is done by a few men and women assembled here below, is registered in the court above. What they have bound on earth is bound in heaven. What they have loosed on earth is also loosed in heaven. It is a happy privilege when they can loose the bound one. When repentance is expressed, when the backslider is restored, when the church has reason to believe that the work of the Spirit is truly in the heart of the offender, then the bond

---

[19] Church Meeting September 5, 1861, *Church Meeting Minutes 1861–1866 Metropolitan Tabernacle*, Metropolitan Tabernacle Archives, London.

is loosed on earth, and it is also loosed in heaven. The meetings of God's servants for the necessary discipline of the church are not trifling meetings, but there is a divine power in them, since what they do is done in the name of Jesus Christ their Lord. Oh, that church meetings were more generally looked at in this solemn light![20]

Any authority exercised by the congregation can only be exercised under Christ's authority. Unlike the Roman Catholic Church, Spurgeon did not believe that excommunication was infallible or condemned anyone to hell. The congregation could get things wrong. At the same time, Christ has given the keys of the kingdom to the church. When practiced "according to Christ's rule," church discipline reflects what takes place in heaven.

Discipline cases during the first seven years of Spurgeon's ministry included instances of embezzlement, abandonment, sexual impropriety, adultery, lying, neglect of religious duties, theft, immorality, and spousal abuse. On one painful occasion, Spurgeon led the congregation in disciplining an elder in the church who had fallen into lust and drunkenness.

Discipline existed not only for moral sins but also doctrinal errors. The church did not discipline over secondary doctrines. Members could resign in good standing if they had changed their position on infant baptism or closed communion. But if a member changed their position on a primary doctrine, the church could excommunicate. Of course, there were always gray areas. On one occasion, Spurgeon warned a member who began holding to annihilationism to find "a more congenial fellowship" where his views

---

[20] *MTP* 30:37.

were held. If he would not do so, "our discipline must take its usual course."[21]

What was the process of church discipline at the Metropolitan Tabernacle? Spurgeon believed that when serious, unrepentant sin was discovered, the church should follow the steps laid out in Matthew 18:15–17.[22] While Matthew 18 provided basic guidelines for church discipline, the process still required wisdom. In some cases, the elders discovered serious sin as they investigated a case of non-attendance, or a member of the church might bring something to the elders. In at least one case, a member of the church was involved in a scandal that was first reported by the press, and the church had to take swift action.

Whichever way a discipline case began, the elders were always eventually involved in the investigation. Members were encouraged to care for one another and to confront serious, unrepentant sins. But if there was no response, the next step would be to bring two or three along. If they were not already involved, the elders would usually be brought in during this step. The elder meeting minutes reveal many discussions regarding cases of church discipline. Multiple elders were usually involved so that multiple witnesses could be established.

---

[21] *Autobiography* 4:125.

[22] "It is a case of discipline. A brother has trespassed against another brother. The offended one has sought him out privately, and by personal expostulation has endeavored to bring him to a better mind; but he has failed. He has then taken with him two or three brethren of the church, and they have together pleaded with the offender that he would do that which is right, but he is obstinate; even in the presence of two or three witnesses he persists in his trespass, and refuses to be won over by kindly entreaty. It only remains that they shall tell it to the church. The church is grieved; it hears the case patiently, and waits upon God in prayer. It asks guidance, and, at last, finding that there is no help for it, removes the member of the body who is not in true sympathy with the rest, and is acting as if he had not the life of God in him." *MTP* 30:37.

If the member continued to be unresponsive to the elders' entreaties, the congregation would eventually see a recommendation for discipline. When presenting a discipline case before the church, the elders sought transparency while also not divulging too much detail which might prove harmful for the church or the individual under discipline. In such instances, the elders called on the congregation to trust their leaders. After the case was presented, a messenger (usually one or two elders) would be formally assigned by the congregation to meet one more time with the unrepentant member.

At a future church meeting, the messenger would report back to the congregation and if there was still no repentance, the church would vote to excommunicate the member. Cases of church discipline at the Tabernacle were typically slow, partly because of the size of the church but also to allow time for repentance. Rarely, but in some cases of public and scandalous sin, the congregation voted on a discipline case at the same meeting where they first heard about it.

Out of all the people that Spurgeon took into membership, less than 2 percent were excommunicated by the church. That's not an insignificant number, but it does reveal that the elders were careful in bringing people into the church. Spurgeon once stated that he knew of "a church which excommunicated eighty members in twelve months, for disorderly conduct and forsaking the truth." That same church took into membership about a hundred new members the prior year, but clearly, they were influenced more by revivalism than any real conversion.[23]

This was not the case at the Metropolitan Tabernacle. Writing in 1865, Spurgeon praised God for how few cases of discipline they had encountered, even though they had taken so many into

---

[23] *NPSP* 2:76.

membership. This was evidence that their ministry was blessed by God.

> Out of the vast numbers who have been added to this Church, how few, happily, how few has God permitted to fall into gross sin or outward backsliding! We have not built a wall which the foxes have broken down. Our ministry has not nourished gourds, which come up in a night and perish in a night, but in the midst of temptations sore, and trials many, all the defections which we have had to mourn over have been but as the small dust of the balance compared with the many who have been kept by the power of divine grace. If the Lord has done all this for us, shall we not delight to honor him?[24]

Conclusion

Pastors, church leaders, when was the last time you looked at your church's membership roll? Do you know these people? Could you give an account for their spiritual condition? Are they walking with the Lord? Are they even alive? Do they attend regularly? More than attending, are they involved in the church? And beyond the church leaders, does the congregation have an awareness of their membership in the church and responsibility for one another?

Undoubtedly, pastoral ministry is daunting. Whether a church of 5,000 or 15, it is an awesome thing to shepherd Christ's flock. Still, this is our calling. As the apostle Peter writes, "Shepherd God's flock among you, not overseeing out of compulsion but willingly, as God would have you; not out of greed for money but eagerly; not

---

[24] *S&T* 1865:6.

lording it over those entrusted to you, but being examples to the flock."[25]

Spurgeon sought to be faithful in this. This chapter has provided an overview of many of his strategies for caring for a church of 5,000. Much of what he did may not be applicable in your context. Likely, churches today would not be well-served by communion tickets or dividing by districts or expiring membership cards. We will have to think for ourselves how to pursue meaningful church membership in the twenty-first century. However, in his commitment to pastoral care, in his practice of church discipline, and in his vision for congregational involvement, we see in Spurgeon biblical principles that we can learn and emulate.

---

[25] 1 Peter 5:2–3

6

THE CHURCH'S
VALIANT SONS
ELDERS AND DEACONS

Needing Help

When Spurgeon arrived at the New Park Street Chapel in 1853, there were a few dozen in attendance and four deacons serving the church. The church was dying. One deacon had just written their annual report to the Baptist Union reporting "no additions to our numbers in consequence of our being without a Pastor." He concluded with this plea, "Brethren, pray for us."[1]

If there were any praying for the ministry at New Park Street, the Lord soon answered their prayers. By the next spring, the church would call Spurgeon to serve as their pastor, and right away, the congregation saw growth. The members of the church were thrilled with the young preacher and invited their neighbors to hear him preach. Members who had stopped attending began to return, curious to hear the new pastor. As word got out about the "boy preacher from the Fens" who had come to London, larger and larger crowds turned out to hear him preach.

The problem of space vexed Spurgeon. The auditorium seated about a thousand, but the church soon outgrew that. Before

---

[1] *Autobiography* 1:340.

safety codes, people crammed into every crack and crevice to hear Spurgeon. The building grew dangerously crowded. By spring of 1855, the deacons had to not only devise a plan for expanding the auditorium, but also coordinate new venues for Sunday gatherings. As Spurgeon preached in larger venues, like Exeter Hall, more and more came out to hear him, so that when they returned to their enlarged building, it was like trying "to put the sea into a teapot."

More than just needing space for attenders, the church saw people converted. Each month, dozens were being baptized and joining the church. As a result, Spurgeon's and his deacons' pastoral workload multiplied. There were interviews to conduct, people to pastor, new believers to disciple, and ministries to organize. It was more than five men could handle. In January 1856, Spurgeon led the church in calling two new men to serve as deacons. This would hardly meet the challenge of growth. At that time, membership of the church was at 595. By January 1857, it had grown to 860. A year later, membership reached 1046. In less than four years, it tripled.

Amid all the growing pastoral and administrative challenges, the deacons began to organize plans for a new building that would seat more than 5,000. The deacons were swamped, and Spurgeon was overworked and beginning to grow ill. Something needed to change, or the church wouldn't survive. As Spurgeon saw his situation, he knew he needed elders alongside him to care for the church.

In this chapter, we will consider Spurgeon's view of church officers—pastors, elders, and deacons. What were their responsibilities? How are they to relate to the congregation? And what encouragement would Spurgeon have for church leaders today?

Implementing Elders

From its earliest days under Benjamin Keach, the church had elders serving alongside the pastor. But in later years, Baptist churches, including New Park Street, began moving away from elders, in part due to their rejection of the Presbyterian model of creating separate offices for teaching and ruling elders. By Spurgeon's time, the New Park Street chapel had one pastor, functioning as the sole elder, alongside a group of deacons. As Spurgeon faced the growing pastoral workload, he knew that the answer was to re-institute a plurality of elders who would give attention to the spiritual care of the church.

One could think that Spurgeon's desire to implement elders was purely pragmatic. But as Spurgeon looked at the New Testament, he was convinced that this arrangement was the New Testament model, with deacons attending "to all secular matters" and elders devoting themselves "to the spiritual part of the work."[2]

How did Spurgeon make the transition? He taught. But he didn't preach a topical sermon calling the church to appoint elders. Rather, as he preached weekly, he searched for opportunities to talk about the office and work of elders. For example, Spurgeon picked Scripture readings in the service that contained references to elders, and highlighted those references in his expositions. On other occasions, he made sermon applications that discussed the work of elders. Preaching in 1857 on Christ's command to feed his sheep, Spurgeon charged his congregation,

> There are more than a hundred young people
> in this church who positively, though they are

---

[2] "When I came to New Park Street, the church had deacons, but no elders; and I thought, from my study of the New Testament, that there should be both orders of officers. They are very useful when we can get them,—the deacons to attend to all secular matters, and the elders to devote themselves to the spiritual part of the work; this division of labor supplies an outlet for two different sorts of talent, and allows two kinds of men to be serviceable to the church; and I am sure it is good to have two sets of brethren as officers, instead of one set who have to do everything, and who often become masters of the church, instead of the servants, as both deacons and elder I should be." *Autobiography* 3:22.

> members, ought not to be left alone; but some of
> our elders, if we have elders, and some who ought
> to be ordained elders, should make it their busi-
> ness to teach them further, to instruct them in the
> faith, and so keep them hard and fast by the truth
> of Jesus Christ. If we had elders, as they had in all
> the apostolic churches, this might in some degree
> be attended to. But now the hands of our deacons
> are full, they do much of the work of the eldership,
> but they cannot do any more than they are doing,
> for they are toiling hard already.[3]

Notice that Spurgeon did not want his people to wait for elders to be appointed. Rather, those in the church who had the gift of eldering ("some of our elders, if we have elders") should begin caring for the church, even if they hadn't been officially ordained yet. He also expressed his conviction that the church would be served by recognizing the elders in her midst.

Over time, this teaching began to take root. Members began to see that the office of elders was biblical and could prove to be a great help to the church.[4] Even though Spurgeon needed help and was convinced that this was scripturally the right step, he did not push for this change but patiently taught on it until there was a groundswell of congregational support. For those familiar with the Baptist denomination, this would've been a significant departure from the common practice of other Baptist churches. But it appears that these members did not hold tightly to tradition. Rather, they

---

[3] *NPSP* 3:86.

[4] "One and another of the members began to inquire of me, 'Ought no we, as a church, to have elders? Cannot we elect some of our brethren who are qualified to fill the office?' I answered that we had better not disturb the existing state of affairs; but some enthusiastic young men said that they would propose at the church meeting that elders should be appointed." *Autobiography* 3:22.

saw a plurality of elders clearly taught from Scripture and wanted to be obedient.

With the support of the congregation, Spurgeon eventually took the lead. On January 12, 1859, the minutes books record the following,

> Our Pastor, in accordance with a previous notice, then stated the necessity that had long been felt by the church for the appointment of certain brethren to the office of elders, to watch over the spiritual affairs of the church. Our Pastor pointed out the Scripture warrant for such an office, and quoted the several passages relating to the ordaining of elders: Titus 1:5, and Acts 14:23;— the qualifications of elders: 1 Timothy 3:1–7, and Titus 1:5–9;—the duties of elders: Acts 20:28–35, 1 Timothy 5:17, and James 5:14; and other mention made of elders: Acts 11:30; 15:4, 6, 23; 16:4, and 1 Timothy 4:14.
>
> Whereupon, it was resolved,—That the church, having heard the statement made by its Pastor respecting the office of the eldership, desires to elect a certain number of brethren to serve the church in that office for one year, it being understood that they are to attend to the spiritual affairs of the church, and not to the temporal matters, which appertain to the deacon only.[5]

With the office created by the congregation, they proceeded to unanimously elect nine men to serve as elders, and agreed that the deacons would continue to serve in some spiritual capacity in this

---

[5] *Autobiography* 3:22–23.

time of transition. Over time, the number of elders and deacons grew, and their division of labor was more clearly established. With this new structure, the church was prepared for the tremendous growth in membership and ministry that would come in the next thirty years.

The Unique Role of the Pastor

There were two offices at the Metropolitan Tabernacle: elders and deacons. However, among the elders, one was devoted to the preaching ministry and leadership of the church, namely the pastor. Spurgeon understood that the New Testament did not create a separate office for pastors. He did, however, see that the New Testament hints that one elder in particular played a role in the ministry of the Word. For example, he believed Paul's instructions to Timothy on "how he should behave himself in the church of God, so as to discharge his office as minister, evangelist, and pastor with honor to himself and profit to the people" point in this direction.[6] Spurgeon also interpreted the stars in Christ's right hand in Revelation 1:16 as the preaching elder, or "the ministers whom God used as messengers to the churches, and from the churches to the outlying world."[7] At the same time, Spurgeon did not create two separate offices of teaching elders and ruling elders, but considered all elders as holding the same office.

As we saw previously, Spurgeon believed that the church was to be built on God's Word. Therefore, the pastor, as the main preaching elder, played a unique role in the church. Because of the pastor's responsibility to preach, it was fitting that the church should also be led by the pastor. That's not to say that elders and deacons did not also share in leadership responsibility. But because the pastor

---

[6] *MTP* 24:541.
[7] *MTP* 33:436.

bore the lion's share of preaching, he held a unique influence in the church. His leadership was unavoidable. So rather than shying away from such leadership, Spurgeon encouraged pastors to humbly recognize the role that they play in the church's unity.

As pastor, Spurgeon did not have the luxury of being uninvolved in ministry and working on sermons all week. Rather, he was the *de facto* chair of every committee and institution in the church. Of course, this doesn't mean that he attended every meeting. The deacons and elders gave more direct oversight. But at times, he did attend their annual meeting to hear reports of the good work being done. Spurgeon provided a unifying presence to the ministries of the church. Of course, this kind of influence and authority could be disastrous for a pastor without godly character. Spurgeon advised pastors not to demand such power, but to earn the trust of their congregations by their evident gentleness and godliness.[8] Knowing the tremendous responsibility of the pastoral role, Spurgeon stressed the importance of discerning a divine pastoral call before entering the ministry.

The Call to Pastoral Ministry

Spurgeon had a high view of the calling of pastoral ministry. Speaking to his students, this is how he defined it:

> I do not . . . in this lecture allude to occasional preaching, or any other form of ministry common to all the saints, but to the work and office of the bishopric, in which is included both teaching

---

[8] "It is the duty of the minister to magnify his office . . . which is best done not by assertions of power or complaints of want of influence, but by possessing such personal weight of piety and prudence, zeal, godliness, gentleness, and forbearance, as will inevitably place him in the front in course of time. In the long run, the measure of any man's power and influence is the measure in which he deserves to possess them; and no man is entitled to expect any more." *S&T* 1869:51.

and bearing rule in the Church, which requires the dedication of a man's entire life to spiritual work, and separation from every secular calling (2 Timothy 2:4); and entitles the man to cast himself for temporal supplies upon the church of God, since he gives up all his time, energies, and endeavors, for the good of those over whom he presides.[9]

Spurgeon valued bi-vocational ministers, especially for smaller churches. But he also understood that some men were called by God to devote all their energy to the work of preaching. These men were to serve as pastors in the church. But how did a man know he has been called by God to serve in this way? Given that Spurgeon ran a college for young men training for ministry, this was a question that he was often asked. To answer, he outlined four qualifications for those weighing a call to ministry:

1. There must be "an intense, all-absorbing desire for the work."

Here, Spurgeon is reflecting on Paul's words in 1 Timothy 3:1. It's important to note that his emphasis is not on desiring the office, but the work.

> In order of a true call to the ministry there must be an irresistible, overwhelming craving and raging thirst for telling others what God has done to our own souls. . . . If any student in this room could be content to be a newspaper editor, or a grocer, or a farmer or a doctor, or a lawyer, or a senator, or a king, in the name of heaven and earth let him go his way; he is not the man in whom dwells the

---

[9] *Lectures* 1:28.

Spirit of God in its fulness, for a man so filled with God would utterly weary of any pursuit but that for which his inmost soul pants. If on the other hand, you can say that for all the wealth of both the Indies you could not and dare not espouse any other calling so as to be put aside from preaching the gospel of Jesus Christ, then, depend upon it, if other things be equally satisfactory, you have the signs of this apostleship.[10]

Spurgeon did not see the aspiration in 1 Timothy 3:1 as a passing ambition, but an irresistible desire to preach God's Word. Spurgeon's basic charge to his students was: "If you can do anything else other than pastoring, do it." And if you can't, then you may well have been called of God.

2. "There must be aptness to teach and some measure of other qualities needful for the office of a public instructor."

Spurgeon notes that out of all the qualifications given in 1 Timothy 3, the one that stands out as unique to the elders is that an elder must be able to teach. "Whatever you may know, you cannot be truly efficient ministers if you are not 'apt to teach.'"[11] As we've already seen, Spurgeon knew that at the heart of pastoral ministry was the preaching of the Word. The church is not built apart from God's Word bringing life to God's people. Therefore, pastors should be men who are able to teach God's Word.

Of course, Spurgeon does not downplay the "other qualities needful for the office of a public instructor." One who is merely skillful in teaching and preaching might be a gifted evangelist, but he will not be ready to pastor. For that, one needs to see evidence

---

[10] *Lectures* 1:23.
[11] *Lectures* 2:28.

of godly character and wisdom as found in the list of qualifications in Paul's letters.

3. One "must see a measure of conversion-work going on under his efforts."

The first two qualifications were true for all elders. But this one was true especially for those who desired to serve in vocational pastoral ministry. Spurgeon believed that the call to pastoral ministry to be divinely sealed by God through the salvation of sinners.

> It is a marvel to me how men continue at ease in preaching year after year without conversions. Have they no bowels of compassion for others? No sense of responsibility upon themselves? Dare they, by a vain misrepresentation of divine sovereignty, cast the blame on their Master? Or is it their belief that Paul plants and Apollos waters, and that God gives no increase? Vain are their talents, their philosophy, their rhetoric, and even their orthodoxy, without the signs following. How are they sent of God who bring no men to God?[12]

As we've seen, Spurgeon understood that preaching was an act of complete dependence on God. Only He could bring about salvation. Therefore, to enter pastoral ministry was to enter a work that one cannot do on his own strength. Even as a man aspired to ministry and exhibited the gifts of a pastor, he was still utterly dependent on God to confirm his calling in the conversion of sinners.

---

[12] *Lectures* 1:50.

4. "Your preaching should be acceptable to the people of God."

Finally, rather than rushing into ministry based on one's own ambitions, the aspiring pastor should wait for a pastoral call from a local church. Speaking to a room full of eager young preachers, Spurgeon warned them to be patient.

> God usually opens doors of utterance for those whom he calls to speak in his name. Impatience would push open or break down the door, but faith waits upon the Lord, and in due season her opportunity is awarded her. When the opportunity comes then comes our trial. Standing up to preach, our spirit will be judged of the assembly, and if it be condemned, or if, as a general rule, the church is not edified, the conclusion may not be disputed, that we are not sent of God. The signs and marks of a true bishop are laid down in the Word for the guidance of the church; and if in following such guidance the brethren see not in us the qualifications, and do not elect us to office, it is plain enough that however well we may evangelize, the office of the pastor is not for us.[13]

Spurgeon encouraged his students to root themselves in the ministry of a local church and prove their giftedness in service to the church. Many churches in that day equated college training to a pastoral calling. As a result, "young men who have never preached are set apart to the ministry; those who have never visited the sick, never instructed the ignorant . . . are supposed to be dedicate to the Christian ministry." But for his students, Spurgeon challenged them to test their calling by serving in the church with zeal while

---

[13] *Lectures* 1:29–30.

they were just members. "If he cannot labor in the church before he pretends to be a minister, he is good for nothing."[14]

Associate Pastor

After having brought on elders in January 1859, Spurgeon found that he still needed help. His pastoral and teaching responsibilities were increasing, and he needed someone who could work alongside him in vocational ministry. So, in November 1862, Spurgeon proposed to revive the office of Teacher. This was an office that existed in the earliest days of the church, under Benjamin Keach. A Teacher was called to assist the Pastor, and sometimes, to succeed the Pastor upon his retirement. Spurgeon saw this office as being exactly what he needed. "The Teacher, without dividing the unity of the pastorate, would, in the judgment of our Pastor, be a valuable aid for the edification of the saints in the matter of word and doctrine."[15]

The church approved and called John Collins to serve in the office of Teacher. But by September 1863, John Collins was called to pastor the church at Southampton, and so the congregation released him for that ministry. Then, in March 1864, the church called Thomas Ness to serve as Teacher, but by October 1865, he too was called away to pastor another church. In the meantime, as the church continued to grow, so did Spurgeon's sickness from overwork.

So in October 1867, the elders and deacons brought a motion to the congregation to call James, Spurgeon's younger brother, "to assist our Pastor in any way considered by him most advisable for the advantage of this church" for a trial period of three months.[16] The trial turned out to be a tremendous blessing both to Spurgeon

---

[14] *MTP* 12:412–13.
[15] *Autobiography* 3:28.
[16] Autobiography 3:31.

and the church, so that by January 1868, the church extended a formal call for James to serve as "co-pastor" to his brother.

However, the elders and deacons provided a few clarifications. This title did not mean that James was equal in position with his brother. Spurgeon would still "act among us as though he were the sole Pastor." But next to him, the church would render to James all the respect and authority that was due to a pastor. Spurgeon would also continue to be the main preaching elder of the church. James may be called to relieve him from time to time, but preaching still belonged primarily to his brother. Instead, James was called to support his brother in pastoral work and anything else needed.[17] Finally, the elders made clear that should something happen to Spurgeon, James would not be the automatic successor but would be relieved of his position.

James was thrilled to accept the call and for twenty-four years, he proved to be a tremendous help to his brother. As the younger brother, James did not begrudge Spurgeon's leadership but was able to free him up to focus on his preaching, writing, and leading the Pastors' College. Spurgeon remained involved in the pastoral care of the church, but he was also able to step away from those responsibilities and get rest. As a result, the church remained unified under their pastor and continued to prosper under his ministry.[18]

The Office and Work of the Elders

The church first called nine elders to serve the congregation in 1859. By 1869, there were twenty-three elders serving, and ten years later, there were thirty elders. That number would rise and

---

[17] *Autobiography* 3:33.

[18] In 1891, the church would extend a call to William Stott to serve as assistant pastor, alongside James. Spurgeon was growing sicker during this time and needing to spend more time away. He would die about a year later.

fall over the years, but the church generally had about thirty elders throughout Spurgeon's ministry. From the beginning, elders were appointed for one-year terms. This may seem odd given the importance of their work. Perhaps, the shorter term reflected the congregationalism of the church. Unlike Presbyterian churches, where the elders ruled over the congregation, the Tabernacle was clear that elders served and led under the authority of the congregation. The congregation could easily replace the entire elder board if they wanted to do so. Practically, this arrangement also allowed for greater flexibility in the appointment of elders. If some elders were failing to carry out their duties, a one-year term allowed the other elders to bring in a replacement relatively quickly without embarrassment to the elder stepping down.

As we saw earlier, the elders were devoted to the spiritual care of the church.[19] To help share the pastoral load of a large church, the elders divided the church geographically into districts and assigned an elder to oversee each one. In addition to pastoral work, the elders also participated in various teaching ministries. "Some of the elders have rendered great service to our own church by conducting Bible-classes and taking oversight of several of our home mission stations." The elders were also faithful evangelists, always on the lookout for visitors in the congregation who seemed affected by the

---

[19] "To the elders is committed the spiritual oversight of the church, and such of its concerns as are not assigned to the deacons nor belong to the preacher. The seeing of inquirers, the visiting of candidates for church membership, the seeking out of absentees, the caring for the sick and troubled, the conducting of prayer-meetings, catechumen and Bible-classes for the young men—these and other needed offices our brethren the elders discharge for the church. One elder is maintained by the church for the especial purpose of visiting our sick poor, and looking after the church-roll, that this may be done regularly and efficiently. As a whole we cheerfully bear our testimony to the beneficial working of the system of deaconate and eldership as distinct offices." *S&T* 1869:53.

sermon. One elder earned himself the title of Spurgeon's "hunting dog," because "he [was] always ready to pick up the wounded bird."[20]

Elders' meetings took place at least once a month, usually at the Tabernacle on Mondays before the prayer meeting. Their primary business was to discuss matters of pastoral care. Most meeting minutes contain the elders' reports and discussions on members who needed pastoral attention, usually due to non-attendance but sometimes in cases of discipline. However, occasionally, the elders gathered to pray and discuss matters pertaining to the larger care of the church. For example, in the elder meeting minutes from September 29, 1876, we find the following entry:

> Held at 350 Kensington Road by invitation of Bro. Payne . . . Both Pastors were present, also Deacons [names listed] . . . Elders [names listed] . . .
>
> Some time was spent in prayer by the Senior Pastor & Bro. Court. After which some discussion took place upon the best method of keeping up a constant visitation of the members of the Church. The question was opened by Bro. Elvin, & the Pastor, & several brothers took part in it.
>
> The names of the following members were mentioned as suitable to fill the office of Elder [names listed] . . .
>
> [name listed] Brother Dunn stated that this person continues to attend the Communion, tho his name has been removed. Bro. D. to write him to see Pastor C.H.S.

---

[20] *Autobiography* 3:23.

After spending a very happy evening the brothers
departed about 10 o'clock.[21]

Earlier that year, the membership was reported to be 4,813.
Yet even with so large a church, these thirty-three elders were
interested in discussing "the best method of keeping up a constant
visitation of the members of the Church." It seems that one solution was to appoint more elders, which they discussed. The elders
were also concerned about an ongoing case of church discipline.
Though caring for such a large church was surely daunting, the
elders took seriously their responsibility and sought to do it faithfully and joyfully.

It is evident from the Elders Meeting Minutes that the eldership was characterized by brotherly collegiality, concern for their
people, and prayerful dependence on God. Spurgeon once declared
that "it would have been utterly impossible for that Church to have
existed, except as a mere sham and huge presence, if it had not been
for the Scriptural and most expedient office of the eldership."[22]

The Office and Work of the Deacons

After the appointment of elders, the deacon board also grew.
When Spurgeon first arrived, there were four deacons at the church.
But as the church grew, so did administrative responsibilities. By
1868, the church had ten deacons. Unlike elders, deacons served
lifetime terms. As a result, Spurgeon was slow to propose new deacons and only did so when needed.

There was a clear division of labor between the elders and the
deacons. Elders looked after the spiritual needs of the church, while

---

[21] Elders Meeting Friday September 29, 1876. *Elders Minutes* 1876–1881,
Metropolitan Tabernacle Archives.
[22] *MTP* 7:261.

deacons were devoted to the practical needs of the church.[23] But rather than the deacons serving under the authority of the elders, both groups exercised their own oversight. One reason for this arrangement may have been simply because there was so much for both groups to do! In taking care of the physical needs of the church, the deacons freed up the elders to pastor the church.

The deacons divided the various tasks among themselves and mostly carried out their responsibilities individually. Some of these responsibilities involved recruiting members to serve as "doorkeepers" or assisting with the Lord's Table. One deacon worked with the elders in facilitating church plants "which are springing from our loins." The deacon who served as general treasurer interacted with many parts of the church as he organized the church's finances. In these and many other practical ways, the deacons' selfless service kept this large church and all her institutions running smoothly.

The deacons also served as trustees of the church. This meant that legally, they were responsible for the church's properties. In those days prior to limited liability, the deacons were generally expected to have the financial means to stand behind the church in case of legal actions taken against the church for slander, debts, or other such charges. As a result, the deacons tended to be gentlemen, or established men of some substance and business experience.[24]

---

[23] "Their duties are to care for the ministry, and help the poor of the church, to regulate the finances and take charge of the church's property, seeing to the order and comfort of all worshipping in the place. The work is divided so as to secure the services of all, and prevent the neglect of anything through uncertainty as to the person responsible for its performance. One honored brother is general treasurer, and has been so for many years—long may he be spared to us; another takes all out-door work, repairs of the exterior, keeping the gates, appointing doorkeepers, etc.; another has all indoor repairs; while others watch over the interests of the new churches which are springing from our loins; and one brother as a good steward sees to the arrangement and provision of the weekly communion, and the elements required for the Lord's table; thus with a common council we have separate duties." *S&T* 1869:52.

[24] Many thanks to Hannah Wyncoll for these insights.

But financial means and administrative skill were not enough to qualify one for deaconship. Spurgeon believed that character was the most important qualification. First Timothy 3 lays out the qualifications of a deacon, and Spurgeon saw these qualifications as non-negotiable. At the top of the list of qualifications, Spurgeon believed that deacons were to be men of peace, working for the church's unity, rather than its division. Deacons characterized by such grace "would be sure to rule well, and reduce chaos to order by the mere force of Christian patience."[25] Of course, this didn't mean that a deacon should allow people to take advantage of the church. At times, a deacon must confront and speak firmly. Yet, at the same time, "the kind, gentle, but earnest deacon is invaluable. He is as an angel in the church, and does more than angel's service. Excellent man!"[26]

Deacons also had opportunities for discipleship and other kinds of Word ministry. Deacons are required to "keep hold of the deep truths of the faith with a clear conscience." Therefore, Spurgeon encouraged deacons to use their teaching gifts in their diaconal ministry and beyond. Deacons shouldn't only be administrators. Rather, their practical ministries provided a platform for the gospel. "We like a [deacon] all the more if, like Stephen, he can both care for the widows and preach the gospel. It would be well for our country churches if more of the deacons would exercise their gifts, and keep the village stations supplied with sound doctrine."[27]

Because the deacons mainly carried out their tasks individually, their work didn't require much coordination. They only met as a deacon board on rare occasions to discuss significant administrative matters facing the church. In April 1861, the deacons met to discuss the opening services of the Metropolitan Tabernacle. They planned

---

[25] *S&T* 1880:9.
[26] *S&T* 1880:9.
[27] *S&T* 1880:10.

for security, the cleaning of the building, finances, and other matters. On another occasion, the deacons met to discuss how they could better care for their pastor, who was recovering from illness in France. They suggested ideas like delaying his return to London until May, moving the Monday night prayer meeting to Tuesday nights (so he could rest after a full day of preaching), devising a way for him to be able to leave right after preaching without having to see anyone, and more. Apparently, the deacons' practical care of the church extended even to the practical care of their pastor.

Spurgeon was deeply grateful for these men and their service. While other pastors complained about their deacons, Spurgeon encouraged Christians to see deacons as gifts of Christ. "Deprive the church of her deacons, and she would be bereaved of her most valiant sons; their loss would be the shaking of the pillars of our spiritual house, and would cause a desolation on every side."[28]

Working Together

Spurgeon did not always have easy relationships with his church officers. When he was called by the church, he was a headstrong, nineteen-year-old pastor of a historic church led by four deacons who had their way of doing things. Before he even arrived, a disagreement arose over the issue of ordination. The deacons wanted their new pastor to be ordained by the Baptist association and take the title of "Reverend." Spurgeon, however, believed that his ordination came from the congregation and was content simply being known as their pastor. He was willing to submit to their wishes but expressed his disapproval over these extra-biblical traditions.

Later, as crowds flocked to hear Spurgeon, the auditorium grew dangerously crowded and unbearably hot. He pressed his deacons to open the windows to allow for more fresh air and to make plans for

---

[28] *S&T* 1868:243.

expansion, but they dragged their feet on any changes to their historic building. At times, he lost his patience with his deacons.[29] But Spurgeon also sought to be gracious with them. As financial pressures increased with the construction of the Tabernacle, he understood that the deacons also bore that pressure. On one occasion, Spurgeon asked a deacon how many new members were joining the church that Sunday, and the deacon respond, "Only seven . . . this won't pay, Governor; running all this big place for seven new members in a month!" Spurgeon saw that the deacon was thinking of the church "as a business undertaking," but rather than being offended, he held his tongue.[30]

Despite these growing pains, Spurgeon had a warm and affectionate relationship with his church officers. As they saw Spurgeon's character and wisdom and flourished under his preaching, they naturally grew to trust their pastor and follow his leadership. And Spurgeon himself loved and depended on these co-laborers in the gospel. Even though some of the deacons and elders held titles and were accomplished in business, they all related to one another as brothers on equal footing.

As we saw above, the officers loved Spurgeon and sought to care for him as he spent himself for the church. When he left to recover his health, the elders and deacons cheerfully carried on with the work, urging Spurgeon not to rush back but to take all the time he needed to recover. They wrote to him frequently, updating him on the church and reassuring him that it was doing well. During one bout of sickness, an elder gave this update,

> Your long affliction, and your tedious banishment, have already borne some peaceable fruits. The stable character of your work has been proved. Had

---

[29] *Autobiography* 1:369.
[30] *Autobiography* 3:20.

the church been built on the basis of your popularity as a preacher, the congregations would not
have been so well kept up in your absence; but,
so far from that being the case, the prayer-meetings and the weekly communion services are well
attended, even when the severe weather, had you
been here, would have been sufficient to account
for some deficiencies.[31]

The health and growth of the church during Spurgeon's
absence was evidence that the ministry of the church was not built
on his popularity but on the faithful ministry of the Word. Even as
Spurgeon was disheartened by his illness, he was encouraged to
hear that the ministry carried on in his absence under the leadership of the elders and deacons.

The Duties of the Congregation toward Their Leaders

The officers of the church played a crucial role in the life of the
church but could not do it alone. Spurgeon called on the church to
support their leaders. Firstly, this meant praying for them. When
Spurgeon accepted the call to be the pastor of the New Park Street
chapel, he asked the congregation "to remember me in prayer, that
I may realize the solemn responsibility of my trust. Remember my
youth and inexperience, and pray that these may not hinder my
usefulness."[32] His need for his people's prayers only increased as
the work grew. And this would be true not only for the pastor, but
also for all the elders and deacons.

More than praying for their leaders, church members also
had a responsibility to follow their example in serving the church.

---

[31] *Autobiography* 4:232.
[32] *Autobiography* 1:353.

Spurgeon repudiated the idea that serving should only be done by those with offices and titles. Rather, the work of the church was to be done by the church members. Every man, woman, and child, filled with the Spirit, had a role to play. This was true when it came to caring for the church. "With four thousand two hundred members in one church . . . what can all the elders and deacons do? The only hope for the church is that God will watch over you all, and that you will all watch over one another."[33] Spurgeon also saw the role of members in following their leaders into gospel ministry. Even as the deacons and elders gave themselves to teaching the Word, so should church members look for ways to "speak in public" and "talk of Christ."[34]

Especially when sick, Spurgeon cared that the church did not fail their leaders. They should continue to attend meetings and participate in the ministries of the church in his absence. Spurgeon did not want to hear about people staying away simply because he was not there. "If you stay away, let it be when I am there, but not now. May the Deacons and Elders find themselves at every meeting for worship surrounded by an untiring band of helpers."[35]

Finally, Spurgeon reminded the church of their responsibility to support their pastors financially. This was never something he had to fight strongly. If anything, the church was generous to Spurgeon and urged him to keep more of his money (he regularly gave it away to support the institutions of the church). But among Baptist churches, this was the exception. Baptists, in his day, had reputations of being stingy with their ministers. As one who sent out many of his students to labor in smaller churches and who worked with his wife and other societies to support poor pastors, Spurgeon

---

[33] *MTP* 53:214.
[34] *MTP* 8:508.
[35] *Autobiography* 3:245–46.

was well-aware that many pastors and their families labored under cruel conditions. This was a reproach to many Baptist churches.

Spurgeon saw the financial support of teachers of God's Word clearly commanded in Scripture. Therefore, supporting one's pastor was not optional, but "plainly the duty of Christian people." Writing in his magazine, he called church members to take responsibility for their pastors. "How we wish that in every congregation some one good man or godly woman would have a mission, and that mission the poor pastor's decent maintenance." Even just one member caring for his pastor's support could make a big difference and save the pastor from arguing for his own salary. Rather than worrying whether these pastors were being paid too much, Spurgeon called members to trust the character of their pastor. "Their want does not arise from vice or extravagance; their incomes are well known, and their expenses can be accurately gauged, and hence there is no danger that any will receive too much."[36] If they could not trust their pastor in these matters, then he should not be serving as their pastor.

Spurgeon's Words to Church Officers

Spurgeon also had words for his own officers. As those in leadership, he wasn't afraid to hold them to a higher standard. Often in his sermons, he publicly addressed points of application to his deacons and elders, both honoring them for their service and holding them accountable.

What would Spurgeon have to say to elders and deacons today? As we conclude this chapter, let me offer five exhortations from Spurgeon for those in church leadership today.

---

[36] *S&T* 1880:414.

Beware of Missing Out on the Gospel

There is great need to urge this matter upon official Christians, such as I am, such as my brethren, the deacons and elders, are. If there are any persons who are likely to be deceived, it is those who are called by their office to act as shepherds to the souls of others. Oh, my brethren, it is so easy for me to imagine because I am a minister, and have to deal with holy things, that therefore I am safe. I pray I may never fall into that delusion, but may always cling to the cross, as a poor, needy sinner resting in the blood of Jesus. Brother ministers, coworkers, and officials of the church, do not imagine that office can save you. The son of perdition was an apostle, greater than we are in office, and yet at this hour he is greater in destruction. See to it, ye that are numbered amongst the leaders of Israel, that you yourselves be saved.[37]

See the Spiritual Nature of Your Work

I have seen the deacons go about their business just as orderly, and with as much precision as if they had been mere automatons, and not men with hearts and souls at all. Do you think God will ever bless a church that is like that? Are we ever to take the kingdom of heaven with a troop of dead men? Never! We want living ministers, living hearers, living deacons, living elders, and until we have such men who have got the very fire of life

---

[37] *MTP* 17:427.

burning in their souls, who have got tongues of life, and eyes of life and souls of life, we shall never see the kingdom of heaven taken by storm.[38]

Be Examples to the Flock

My dear brethren in office, my esteemed deacons and elders, I pray that you may have the grace of our Lord Jesus Christ abundantly, so that you may walk before us as becometh fathers in Israel, that you may be ensamples to the flock, that none of the weaker sort may see in you any occasion of stumbling, but much that may lead them forward in the divine life.[39]

Cultivate Contentment in Your Work

And here let me speak to the elders and deacons of this church. Brethren, learn to be content with the office you hold, not envious of any superior honor to exalt yourselves. I turn to myself. I turn to the ministry, I turn to all of us in our ranks and degrees in Christ's Church, we must be content with the honor God is pleased to confer upon us; nay let us think nothing of honor, but be content to give it all up, knowing that it is but a puff of breath after all. Let us be willing to be the servants of the Church, and to serve them for nought, if need be even without the reward of their thanks, may we but receive at last the right good sentence from the lips of the Lord Jesus Christ. We must

---

[38] *MTP* 5:219.
[39] *MTP* 17:249.

learn, in whatever state we are, therewith to be content.[40]

Depend on Christ—It Is His Church, after All!

My brethren, the deacons and elders of the church, must always take comfort from this thought. If there is anything in the church that grieves us, we must feel, "It is his vineyard, not ours; it is before him, so he will know what to do with it." I am sure, dear brethren, we should lay down our tasks if we had not our Master with us. I should not dare to be a minister, and you would not dare to be church-officers, unless we felt that it was before him. In your different districts, let the sick, the sorrowful, the backsliding, all be carried before your God; and let all the members feel that, although we are but feeble creatures to be the leaders of so great a host, yet that the church may grow and increase until we are not only fifteen hundred, but fifteen thousand if the Lord will, and that the church would then be just as carefully looked after as it is now, for it would still, be before him. He who is the Husbandman is just as able to care for his vines when they are most numerous as if there were only one, and that one had the whole of his attention.[41]

[40] *NPSP* 6:273.
[41] *MTP* 48:305–6.

Conclusion

My guess is not all church leaders reading this chapter will find themselves in similar church situations as Spurgeon did. And yet, for many of your situations, I imagine Spurgeon would challenge or encourage you. For those of you who are serving as solo pastors, Spurgeon would challenge you to raise up elders and deacons to work alongside you. For those of you who are experiencing conflict with other church leaders, how can you imitate Spurgeon's example in cultivating patience and collegiality among your ministry team? For those of you who are serving as lay elders alongside a busy pastor, what would it look like to be generous and caring in your support of his ministry? For those of you serving as deacons in the church, how might you take more initiative to free up the pastors to shepherd the congregation?

The Metropolitan Tabernacle was a challenging congregation to pastor. But Spurgeon's ministry is a reminder that the care of the church was never meant to be a solo sport. It is to be accomplished by a team of elders and deacons, who engage and equip the entire church to care for one another. Wherever your starting point, pray and work toward that goal.

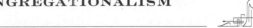

7

THIS MOST
BLESSED MEETING

CONGREGATIONALISM

The Joy of Long Church Meetings

Spurgeon had plenty of responsibilities to keep him busy. He prepared and preached multiple sermons a week. He led Monday night prayer meetings and Sunday and Thursday worship services. He worked with publishers to edit and print weekly sermons. He met with his elders and deacons to care for the church. He conducted membership interviews, wrote multiple books, and led the Pastors' College. And if all that weren't enough, he attended and chaired the church meetings.

What were the church meetings? These were the meetings where the congregation gathered as a church to make decisions about matters of membership, discipline, leadership, and more. Churches today might call them congregational meetings or business meetings. Pastors both today and in the past dreaded these meetings. But Spurgeon saw them as an important part of his ministry and leadership.

He tells the story of a time early on when he left home early in the morning, went to the chapel, and met with membership applicants all day long. "Their stories were so interesting to me that the hours flew by without my noticing how fast they were

going." He estimates he saw over thirty people that day. Soon it
was seven o'clock, which meant it was time for the Monday night
prayer meeting. After that, came the church meeting, which probably began around eight o'clock. Two hours later, Spurgeon began
to feel faint, and only then, he realized that he had not eaten all
day! He recounts, "I never thought of it, I never even felt hungry,
because God had made me so glad and so satisfied with the Divine
manna, the Heavenly food of success in winning souls."[1] Church
meetings were an important part of harvesting "the Divine manna"
of conversions.

We don't know when Spurgeon finally ate that night. But on
another occasion, May 18, 1860, we see recorded in the minute
books that forty-two candidates appeared before the church, each
giving testimony to their conversion. This meeting began at two
o'clock in the afternoon, and according to Spurgeon's notes in the
margin, "This most blessed meeting lasted till a late hour at night.
Bless the Lord." If each candidate took ten minutes to be reported
by the messenger, interviewed by the chair, and voted on by the
congregation, that would still have the meeting lasting until nine
o'clock. Given the need for breaks and for dinner, that memorable church meeting probably ran until eleven or midnight. Note
that these meetings are not just late nights for the pastor. They
involved the whole church! Even so, as the meeting ended late into
the night, the congregation found reason to rejoice. The late hour
represented God's faithfulness in blessing the ministry of the Word.
These church meetings were a source of joy.

This chapter will examine Spurgeon's congregational church
structure, both in his teaching and practice. Last chapter, we saw
the importance of church leaders. But at the end of the day, it was
the congregation that carried the final authority in the church. As

---

[1] *Autobiography* 2:137.

strong of a leader as Spurgeon was, he was nonetheless fully committed to congregational authority. Let's see how this played out in his ministry.

Spurgeon's Teaching on Congregationalism

The starting point for Spurgeon's understanding of church structure was the reign of Christ. Jesus alone rules the church. Therefore, churches are not to be ruled by their pastors, denominations, or congregations, but ultimately by Christ. "There is no place for the reign of autocracy, or aristocracy, or even democracy, in Christ's Churches. His kingdom is a Theocracy, (a Christocracy)."[2] Because Christ alone ruled the church, no person or group can exercise supreme authority over the church. Rather, every congregation, led by the Spirit, should be free to follow Christ's reign, as reflected in the Scriptures. And in the Scriptures, Christ made clear how the church is to be ordered and led.[3]

A few features can be noticed in Spurgeon's understanding of congregational polity. First, "every Church member should have equal right and privileges," particularly in relation to other authorities in the church. The church officers cannot execute anything "unless they have the full authorization" of the members. No leader

---

[2] *S&T* 1865:438–40.

[3] "To our minds, the Scripture seems very explicit as to how this Church should be ordered. We believe that every Church member should have equal rights and privileges; that there is no power in Church officers to execute anything unless they have the full authorization of the members of the Church. We believe, however, that the Church should choose its pastor, and having chosen him, that they should love him and respect him for his work's sake; that with him should be associated the deacons of the Church to take the oversight of pecuniary matters; and the elders of the Church to assist in all the works of the pastorate in the fear of God, being overseers of the flock. Such a Church we believe to be scripturally ordered; and if it abide in the faith, rooted, and grounded, and settled, such a Church may expect the benediction of heaven, and so it shall become the pillar and ground of the truth." *MTP* 7:362.

carries more votes in church matters than any other member of the church. In the end, the members collectively exercise final authority in the church. Second, these congregations should be led by church officers—the pastor, elders, and deacons—and the congregation should love and respect them. While the congregation holds ultimate authority, they should honor their shepherds and follow their leadership. Finally, none of this was mere pragmatism, but Spurgeon saw this form of church officer-led congregationalism as "very explicit" in Scripture. Churches that abided by this pattern would not only be blessed, but would proclaim and protect the gospel.

Though Spurgeon held to his views from Scripture, he still appreciated something in every type of church polity. The Presbyterians "put an elder in every corner" and organized their Presbytery as "the great ground-work," and they were right in doing so "to an extent." The Episcopalians "will have a bishop at the door-post" and they organize their church "according to the model that was seen by Cranmer in the mount." And Baptists, of course, have "a simpler style" with "every congregation distinct and separate, and governed by its own bishop, and deacons, and elders."[4] Amid these differences, it was important for evangelical churches not to disfellowship one another over church polity, but to work together for unity. Christ's reign extends beyond Baptists to all the churches. Even if some have erred in their structure, nonetheless, Christ owns them as they hold on to the gospel.

In his own polity, Spurgeon saw something of an amalgamation of various polities. Speaking at the opening of the Metropolitan Tabernacle, he declared "that a modified form of Episcopalian Presbyterian Independency is the Scriptural method of Church government; at any rate, no other form of government would have worked in so large a church as this."[5] Even though he was Baptist,

---

4 *NPSP* 4:212.
5 *MTP* 7:257.

he had no problems making "Presbyterian alliances," i.e., participating in local and national associations to cooperate for the gospel. Not only that, but the church was shepherded by a plurality
of elders, a feature of Presbyterian churches and a rarity among
Baptists in Spurgeon's day. As the pastor of a large congregation
with elders and deacons and multiplying institutions, Spurgeon
saw aspects of Episcopalian polity in the influence of his leadership.
There was much to learn from all these different models, but in
the end, the Metropolitan Tabernacle held to the Independency, or
congregationalism, of the local church.

> The Church of Christ meeting here is within itself
> a family, that it is whole and entire and needs
> nothing from without to make it complete. We do
> not for instance, need to appeal to a synod, or to a
> general assembly. We do not look up to one minis-
> ter called a bishop, or to some other person called
> an archbishop. The Church has its own bishop or
> pastor; it has its own presbytery or elders; it has
> its own deaconship, and is not therefore depen-
> dent on any other, but should every other Church
> become extinct its organization would not be
> marred.[6]

It was this conviction about the church that provided the basis
for their church meetings.

Church Meetings at the Tabernacle

At a special church meeting on April 19, 1854, the congregation
of the New Park Street Chapel passed the unanimous resolution to

---

[6] *MTP* 7:257.

"tender our Brother the Revd. C. H. Spurgeon a most cordial and affectional invitation forthwith to become Pastor of this Church."[7] James Low, the chairman of the deacons, informed Spurgeon of the call the next day and added, "If you feel it your duty to accept the invitation of the Church to become its Pastor, it will be desirable that you should obtain your dismission from the Church at Waterbeach to our Church as early as you can, in order that you may be in a position as a member to attend our church meetings."[8] The church received Spurgeon's acceptance on May 5 (along with his dismission from Waterbeach Chapel), and by May 17, he would preside over his first church meeting as the pastor of the church.

Over the course of his ministry, the church would hold 1,862 church meetings to conduct the business of the church. This would average out to nearly fifty church meetings per year. Before Spurgeon's arrival in 1854, the church held meetings once a month. However, by the fall of 1855, the congregation met twice a month in order to receive all the visitors applying for membership. The following year, the congregation held thirty church meetings, almost twice as the previous year. The move to the Metropolitan Tabernacle in 1861 brought an increase in membership applications, more than doubling the number from previous years. For the next thirty years, the congregation would hold around sixty church meetings a year, and at times, more than eighty church meetings a year.

At first, the church held monthly church meetings on Wednesday nights. But as they grew more frequent, the church began holding church meetings before and after other gatherings of the church (i.e., the Monday night prayer meeting and Thursday night service), since the church had already gathered. This allowed

---

[7] Special Adjourned Church Meeting Wednesday April 19, 1854, *Church Meeting Minutes 1808–1854 Tooley Street & Carter Lane*, Metropolitan Tabernacle Archives, London.

[8] *Autobiography* 1:351.

the church to hold at least eight church meetings a month, without having to gather on any additional evenings.

How well attended were these meetings? After the construction of the Tabernacle in 1861, church meetings usually took place in the lecture hall underneath the auditorium, which seated nearly 900 people. Commenting on space, Spurgeon said, "The lecture-hall, beneath this platform, is for our church meetings; it is rendered fully necessary, as we have now more than 1,500 members."[9] It appears by that comment that the lecture hall was filled for church meetings by that point, with nearly 2/3 of the congregation regularly attending those meetings. As the church grew, they would eventually move their church meetings to the main auditorium.

As busy as he was, Spurgeon was committed to being at these church meetings. In the first nine years of his ministry, he attended and chaired every church meeting, 267 in all. But as his health faltered and his responsibilities continued to grow, Spurgeon had to learn to lean on others. Beginning in 1863, Spurgeon allowed his deacons and elders to chair church meetings when he was unavailable. In 1868, with the arrival of James, Spurgeon would turn this responsibility almost entirely over to his associate pastor. With some exceptions, the church meetings would be chaired by James going forward.

However, there was one church meeting for which Spurgeon always tried to be present, namely the annual meeting. This typically took place at the beginning of the year, and all members were encouraged to be present. It included a church-wide afternoon tea, which was a rich time of fellowship for the members. Then, the meeting would begin around 6:30 p.m. Its highlights would include reports on the previous year's finances and membership growth, the election of new elders and deacons, various comments by the

---

[9] *Autobiography* 2:356.

pastor, and reports from the various institutions of the church. On
Wednesday, February 18, 1880, the congregation gathered for their
annual meeting, and the following report was published,

> About eighteen hundred of the members were
> present to tea, and a much larger number assem-
> bled afterwards. It was a most delightful evening,
> full of affection and enthusiasm. Speech is free,
> and affection has greater liberty at a select meet-
> ing. . . . The pastor's spirits were raised, and his
> heart cheered by the loving words of his officers
> and people, and all were happy and grateful to
> God. The financial accounts were exceedingly
> satisfactory, especially when we remember what
> a trying year 1879 has been in this respect to all
> institutions. Nothing is lacking to any branch of
> church work. All that is needed is a continuance
> of the blessing, and more grace.[10]

Church meetings were important to the life of the Metropolitan
Tabernacle. Sunday worship services were devoted to corporate worship. Thursday night services provided a midweek gathering around
God's Word. Monday prayer meetings reminded the congregation
of their dependence on God. And church meetings were a joyful
reminder of God's faithfulness in blessing their ministry.

Ordering a Church Meeting

Not all pastors shared the same joyful outlook regarding
church meetings. Church meetings had a bad reputation. Spurgeon
lamented, "We are afraid that there are churches still in existence

---

[10] *S&T* 1880:140.

where every church meeting is anticipated with anxiety lest it should be made a season of debate." Too often, they were marked by church feuds, doctrinal disagreements, and opposition to leadership. As Spurgeon observed these challenges, he believed that a church's disunity ultimately limited its fruitfulness. "Under such conditions edification may be sighed for in vain, and the conversion of sinners may be regarded as most improbable."[11]

Therefore, an important part of pastoral ministry was knowing how to lead church meetings well. Leadership was so important that even though these meetings were familial and intimate, Spurgeon still approached each meeting well-prepared and depended on the Holy Spirit for the right words.[12] But beyond prayerful dependence on the Spirit, how did Spurgeon order his church meetings to promote the unity of the church?

Prioritizing the Work of the Church

Spurgeon tells the story of one "much-tried brother minister" asking a former pastor of his church, "How is it, Doctor, that your church is always so peaceful?" The wise pastor responded, "You see, we don't call a church meeting to consult about buying a new broom every time we want one, and we don't entreat every noisy member to make a speech about the price of the soap the floors are scrubbed with."[13] Maintaining the unity of the church often meant discerning

---

[11] *S&T* 1877:148.

[12] "I love to preach in such a mood, not as though I was about to preach at all, but hoping that the Holy Spirit would speak through me. Thus to conduct prayer-meetings, and church meetings, and all sorts of business, will be found to be our wisdom and our joy. We generally make our worst blunders about things that are perfectly easy, when the thing is so plain that we do not ask God to guide us, because we think our own common sense will be sufficient, and so we commit grave errors; but in the difficulties, the extreme difficulties, which we take before God, He gives young men prudence, and teaches youths knowledge and discretion. Dependence upon God is the flowing fountain of success." *AARM* 191.

[13] *Autobiography* 1:312–13.

which decisions should be brought before the congregation, and which ones should be handled by the leaders of the church. So, what did the congregation at the Tabernacle vote on?

Church Membership

Membership additions. The main reason for the increase in church meetings was due to the increase in membership applicants. Spurgeon committed to having the congregation be the final authority in matters of church membership. Even as applicants increased, he refused to take shortcuts in the membership process. It would have been much easier for the elders to approve applicants into membership directly. They conducted membership interviews, and the congregation only acted on their recommendation. Spurgeon, however, remained committed to the congregation's authority when it came to membership. In bringing applicants into membership, the congregation expressed their commitment to care for each new member. This commitment was also pictured in the Lord's Supper, as the church extended the right hand of fellowship to new members.

Membership removals. The congregation also determined the removal of members. Membership meant accountability to the church. Other than deaths, removal from the membership roll required a congregational action. From the removal of inactive members to dismissals, to every case of church discipline, all removals required a congregational vote and all of them carried the weight of the entire congregation.

Calling Elders and Deacons

At every annual meeting, one agenda item was the election of new church officers. Deacons held lifetime terms and would only be voted on at the beginning of their term. As the work grew, Spurgeon slowly added more deacons so that by the end of his ministry, there were twenty-one deacons serving the church. Elders, on the other hand, held one-year terms. Every annual meeting, the congregation voted on a full slate of elders. They also voted on any deacons who would serve in dual-capacity as deacon-elders. Not counting any dual-capacity deacons, Spurgeon began with nine elders in 1859. By 1873, that number would grow to twenty-eight. Spurgeon would average about thirty elders each year from then (again, not counting any deacons serving in dual capacity).

How were new deacons or elders nominated? Any member could nominate an officer at a church meeting, but I'm not aware of this ever happening. Instead, the pastor, on behalf of the elders, brought recommendations at the annual meeting for any elder or deacon nominations. Throughout the year, Spurgeon and the elders were always looking out for those serving faithfully in the congregation. They also evaluated existing elders and deacons to see if they were fulfilling their office. As the annual meeting approached, they discussed what they observed and finalized their list of nominations. Spurgeon writes,

> I have always made it a rule to consult the existing officers of the church before recommending the election of new deacons or elders, and I have also been on the lookout for those who have proved their fitness for office by the work they have accomplished in their private capacity.[14]

They did not require total unanimity for a nomination, but there still had to be a "general unanimity" among elders.

Then, the names would be presented to the congregation at the annual meeting. They would discuss the names, and a vote would be taken. One interesting feature is that during the vote,

---

[14] *Autobiography* 3:23.

the congregation might have sung a hymn that was written by Spurgeon for these occasions.

> [1] Risen Lord, Thou hast received
> Gifts to bless the sons of men,
> That with souls who have believed,
> God might dwell on earth again.
>
> [2] Now these gifts be pleased to send us,
> Elders, deacons still supply,
> Men whom Thou art pleased to lend us,
> All the saints to edify.
>
> [3] Guide us while we here select them,
> Let the Holy Ghost be nigh,
> Do Thou, Lord, Thyself elect them,
> And ordain them from on high.
>
> *[Pause while the election is made.]*
>
> [4] Lord, Thy church invokes Thy blessing
> On her chosen {elders' / deacons'} head,
> Here we stand our need confessing,
> Waiting till Thy grace be shed
>
> [5] Pour on them Thy rich anointing,
> Fill Thy servants with Thy power
> Prove them of Thine own appointing,
> Bless them from this very hour.[15]

Even while holding the final say, the congregation was happy to entrust the work of evaluating and nominating leaders to their

---

[15] C. H. Spurgeon, *Our Own Hymn-Book: A Collection of Psalms and Hymns for Public, Social, and Private Worship* (London: Passmore & Alabaster, 1885), hymn 904.

existing leaders. During Spurgeon's ministry, the congregation never dissented from their pastor's nominations.

For those committed to congregationalism, such a process might appear to be too authoritarian and not democratic enough. However, Spurgeon understood the challenge for a congregation to adequately evaluate their own members. Some congregational churches adopted open elections, which led to confusion. He tells the story of one church that printed the names of all the male members and asked the members to vote on a certain number by ballot. "A very old man was within two or three votes of being elected simply because his name began with A, and therefore was put at the top of the list of candidates."[16] In a church as large as the Tabernacle, the elders *needed* to lead in this process. Their leadership did not compromise their convictions but preserved both the authority and unity of the church.[17]

Calling a Pastor

The first debate that Spurgeon had with one of his deacons was over ordination. Shortly after his arrival, an aged deacon wanted the nineteen-year-old pastor to be publicly recognized by the other Baptist churches through an ordination service. According to custom, this involved pastors of other churches in the denomination examining the new pastor on his theology and ministry philosophy. There would likely be a dinner where speeches would be made, and advice would be given to the new pastor. After the ordeal, the pastor would be formally ordained and given the title of "Reverend."

Spurgeon found all of this to be unbiblical and contradictory to the principles of congregationalism. He wrote to his deacon,

---

[16] *Autobiography* 3:23.
[17] *S&T* 1869:52–53.

I believe in the glorious principle of Independency. Every church has a right to choose its own minister; and if so, certainly it needs no assistance from others in appointing him to the office. You, yourselves, have chosen me; and what matters it if the whole world dislikes the choice? They cannot invalidate it; nor can they give it more force. It seems to me that other ministers have no more to do with me, as your minister, than the crown of France has with the crown of Britain. We are allies, but we have no authority in each other's territories. They are my superiors in piety, and other personal matters; but, ex officio, no man is my superior. We have no apostles to send Titus to ordain. Prelatic power is gone. All we are brethren.[18]

The church did not need permission from an ordination council to call their pastor. Certainly, there was a place for seeking advice or for other churches to formally recognize a new pastor. But each congregation had the authority to complete the work of calling and ordaining their own pastors. Rather than any elaborate process, "the ordination prayer should be prayed in the church meeting, and there and then the work [is] done."[19]

---

[18] *Autobiography* 1:357.
[19] "We offer no opinion here as to other methods of electing church officers, but we will add that no other plan commends itself so much to our judgment; no other plan is so safe for our church, or so likely to procure good officers. No other plan is so helpful to the pastor, who is most concerned in the choice, having to work with those selected; and no other plan as we can see will enable him so faithfully to discharge his office of guide and shepherd, in one of the most critical periods of the church's history. Timidity here is a crime, and the affectation of modesty in not wishing to influence the church is to our mind dereliction of duty. A church possessed of unlimited liberty of action, needs, for the sake of its junior and less instructed members, to be directed in its choice of officers—the best men

The Ministry of the Church

The congregation also voted on significant matters regarding the ministry of the church. A survey of the first seven years of church meetings after Spurgeon's arrival shows the church voting on building projects, messengers for associational meetings, the collection of special offerings, benevolence for needy members, public statements about the ministry of the church and their pastor, gifts to other churches, and special seasons of prayer. With all these, Spurgeon understood that the church's ministry could not happen apart from the congregation and he involved them in these decisions through church meetings.

One striking example of congregational involvement was in the matter of buildings and worship venues. The congregation not only voted on the expansion of the New Park Street Chapel and the construction of the Metropolitan Tabernacle, but they also voted on various arrangements for venues that were made in the preceding years. On May 26, 1856, we find the following motion in the meeting minutes, "Resolved,—That arrangements be made, as early as possible, for this church to worship at Exeter Hall on the Sabbath evenings during the Summer months." Exeter Hall was a large venue used by evangelical groups for religious and philanthropic gatherings. Even though it was unusual for a church to use it for worship services, the venue still had religious connections, making it acceptable.

But later that fall, another motion was passed,

> This meeting was convened to consider the propriety of engaging the use of the large hall in the Royal Surrey Gardens for our Sabbath evening worship, the directors of Exeter Hall having refused the

---

to do it are the pastor and officers already tried and proved, and the fear of giving offence seems to us but the fear of man which bringeth a snare." *S&T* 1874:266.

church the further use of that place. After several
of the brethren had expressed their concurrence,
it was resolved that the Music Hall of the Royal
Surrey Gardens be engaged for one month, com-
mencing the third Sabbath in October.[20]

Some historians note that Spurgeon showed innovation in his
use of secular venues for religious gatherings. In his day, it would
have been unthinkable for a church to hold services in a music hall.
And yet, for many who never attended a regular church gathering,
those services at the Surrey Gardens were their first exposure to the
gospel. Indeed, this was a bold step in Spurgeon's ministry.

It is worth noting, however, that Spurgeon did not decide this
unilaterally. Undoubtedly, he led the church in this decision. But
this was also discussed in the congregation as they considered "the
propriety of engaging the use of the large hall in the Royal Surrey
Gardens for our Sabbath evening worship." In the end, this significant ministry decision was made, not just by the pastor or the deacons, but by the church. Even as onlookers disapproved, the church
was united in this important decision.

Maintaining Order

For a congregation to discuss and vote on important matters,
their meetings needed to be organized. How did Spurgeon maintain
order in his church meetings?

First, a recognized chair led each meeting. As has been noted,
this position was always filled by Spurgeon, his co-pastor, James, or,
at times, a long-standing elder or deacon in the church. In other
words, the chair was always filled by someone who was known by the
congregation and commanded the respect of the people. The chair
set the agenda of the meeting, welcomed participants, arranged for

---

[20] *Autobiography* 2:199.

the opening prayer, stated the meeting objectives, managed discussions, kept the meeting moving, and concluded the meeting at the appropriate time.

But in the context of a church meeting, the chair could also use the various events or difficulties in the life of the church to teach and shepherd the congregation. Every moment was a teaching opportunity. He might lead in impromptu prayers, call the congregation to greater faith, or remind them of their vision for the ministry. Much of this could happen spontaneously. Therefore, Spurgeon recognized the need to depend on the Spirit for wisdom while chairing these meetings.

Second, rather than being an "ecclesiastical bear-garden," church meetings were guided by rules. Churches often conducted their meetings informally because everyone knew each other and assumed that everything would be fine. But this only led to conflict. Therefore, Spurgeon encouraged pastors to lead their congregations in adopting rules to govern meetings. "The ordinary rules of public meetings are the best guide for the chairman of a church meeting, and should not be disregarded." Robert's Rules of Order would not be written until 1876. Nevertheless, there were plenty of other sources that offered rules for running a meeting. Spurgeon didn't care which rules were used so long as they made common sense and promoted order. "Where reason suffices revelation is not to be expected."[21]

One important rule that Spurgeon adopted is that he would not allow members to raise motions or discussions in a church meeting without prior notice. He tells this painful anecdote,

> We remember an instance in which, before much
> of the fit business of the assembly had been trans-
> acted, a member suddenly proposed a resolution,

---

[21] *S&T* 1872:200.

or rather raved out a denunciation concerning the sacramental wine; he was followed by a second, who wished to abolish pew-rents, and he by a third reformer, who wanted meetings where everybody could speak as some sort of spirit might move him; and, when the third sat down, a fourth advocated the frequent change of deacons, hinting that those in office had lost the confidence of the members. The church was so worn and harassed with impromptu suggestions of this kind, that both pastor and people abhorred the very name of church meeting and suddenly discovered that, for the protection of the quiet many, the noisy few ought not to be allowed to ride their various hobbies at pleasure.[22]

Some may see this limitation as overriding the members' authority, but Spurgeon saw this as preserving the interests of the congregation. Any member could propose an item for discussion to one of the deacons or elders. But for an item to be discussed at a church meeting, it had to be vetted by the chair prior to the meeting. Part of the vetting process was determining whether the discussion came "within the province of the assembly." Items that should not be dealt with by the congregation would be declined by the chair. Of course, a member could still choose to be disruptive and raise a discussion point at a meeting, but Spurgeon warned members against such actions. Perhaps a church could find itself under such unbiblical leadership that such an action would be appropriate. But "a member ought to hesitate a long time before he proceeds contrary to the judgment of the officers."[23]

---

[22] *S&T* 1872:200.
[23] *S&T* 1872:201.

Third, the church kept an accurate record of minutes for each meeting. "All minutes of church meetings, deacons' and elders' courts, are entered, and confirmed at the following meeting."[24] The meeting minutes were taken by church members present at the church meeting. They included all the decisions of the congregation, important discussion or information surrounding those decisions, records of correspondence to and from the church, and much more. While nineteenth century London could be litigious, the minute books sought to be both informative and discrete in what was recorded. At the following meeting, the minutes of the previous meeting would be reviewed and confirmed by the meeting chair.

Finally, the leaders cultivated congregational trust in their leadership. This was perhaps the most important ingredient for an orderly meeting. In the use of rules, the keeping of minutes, financial and membership reports, and so much more, Spurgeon's goal was to be transparent and to communicate clearly so that the congregation understood what was going on and could trust their leaders. In the case of finances, "all money matters [were] audited by unofficial brethren selected by the church, and the accounts read and books produced at the annual church meeting." When there were cases where leaders could not be fully transparent for pastoral or legal reasons, they let the congregation know and asked for their trust.

> In all our business the aim is to have everything done openly and aboveboard, so that no one may complain of the existence of a clique, or the suppression of the true state of affairs. We occasionally ask the unquestioning confidence of the church in its officers in cases delicate and undesirable to be

---

[24] *S&T* 1869:151.

published, but otherwise we consult the church in everything, and report progress as often as possible in all matters still pending and unsettled. Nothing, we are persuaded, is so sure to create suspicion and destroy confidence as attempts at secret diplomacy, or mere official action.[25]

Edifying the Congregation

More than just conducting the "business" of the church, Spurgeon saw church meetings as an opportunity for discipleship and edification. Every membership applicant brought a testimony of God's grace with them, and in so many of these testimonies, Spurgeon played only a small part. Rather, applicants told stories of a praying mother, a persevering neighbor, a stranger who invited them to church, a faithful deacon, and all kinds of other ways the members of the church brought them to Christ. Each story encouraged members to be bold in the work of the gospel.

Spurgeon also sought opportunities to point his people to the wider work that was happening in the church. Whether it was sending out new church plants, appointing missionaries, discussing the work of the Pastors' College, honoring faithful leaders, telling stories of enduring fruitfulness, these church meetings provided the congregation an opportunity to celebrate all that God was doing through the church. As a result, the church often voiced their praise to God.

On June 18, 1861, after taking in an unusually large number of new members, the church passed this resolution:

It was unanimously resolved that a record of our gratitude to God for His graciousness toward us should be made in the church-book. With our

---

[25] *S&T* 1869:55.

whole hearts, as a highly favored church and people, we magnify and extol the lovingkindness; of our God in so singularly owning the Word proclaimed among us, by giving so many souls to be added to our number. To God be all the glory! Oh, that we may be more than ever devoted to His honor and service![26]

Conclusion

Many pastors find it difficult to get excited about church meetings. These meetings often end up feeling more bureaucratic than spiritual. Church meetings can sometimes get downright nasty, as members argue and fight over their own preferences. It's no surprise that many pastors find themselves drawn to top-down church government models, rather than congregationalism.

But Spurgeon's example here demonstrates that congregationalism does not have to mean a leader-less democracy. The elders, especially the preaching pastor, play a significant role in guiding and shepherding the church. Even in following the New Testament pattern of congregational rule, we recognize that Christians are called to obey their leaders. Under the wise leadership of elders, church meetings can be marked by order, spiritual edification, and unity.

But this takes wisdom and much prayer. This requires thoughtful leadership and teaching. As you look ahead to your next church meeting, how can you prepare your congregation to understand their role in the church? How can you order that meeting to highlight the work of God in your church and encourage your people? What would it look like for church meetings to become another part of the church's discipleship?

---

[26] *Autobiography* 3:12.

8

A WORKING CHURCH

THE MINISTRY
OF THE CHURCH

"A Greater and Grander Man"

In the fall of 1878, John B. Gough, an American temperance advocate, visited Spurgeon in London. It was a beautiful Saturday and Spurgeon proposed that they visit the orphanage in Stockwell. That afternoon, Gough witnessed a side of Spurgeon that he had never seen before.

Established in 1869, the orphanage rescued hundreds of children from the streets throughout Spurgeon's lifetime. It served children from all kinds of denominational backgrounds—Church of England, Baptist, Congregationalist, Wesleyan, and many more. Many of these children were converted and joined the Tabernacle. Some went on to be trained for ministry in the Pastors' College. But the orphanage was more than just a ministry to Spurgeon. They were family.

His arrival brought a "shout of joy" from the boys "at the sight of their benefactor." Gough described Spurgeon's interactions with the orphans "like a great boy among boys." The most famous preacher in the world now struck Gough with his child-like simplicity among these children. After visiting briefly with the headmaster and giving each boy a shilling, leading to "a shrill hearty hurrah,"

Spurgeon turned his attention to the infirmary. There was an orphan dying of consumption, and Spurgeon knew the boy would be disappointed if he didn't visit him.

> We went into the cool and sweet chamber and there lay the boy. He was very much excited when he saw Mr. Spurgeon. The great preacher sat by his side.'. . . . Holding the boy's hand in his, he said:
>
> "Well, my dear, you have some precious promises in sight all around the room. Now, dear, you are going to die, and you are very tired lying here, and soon you will be free from all pain, and you will rest. Nurse, did he rest last night?"
>
> "He coughed very much."
>
> "Ah, my dear boy, it seems very hard for you to lie here all day in pain, and cough all night. Do you love Jesus?"
>
> "Yes."
>
> "Jesus loves you. He bought you with His precious blood, and He knows what is best for you. It seems hard for you to lie here and listen to the shouts of the healthy boys outside at play. But soon Jesus will take you home, and then He will tell you the reason, and you will be so glad."
>
> Then, laying his hand on the boy, without the formality of kneeling, he said, "O Jesus, Master, this dear child is reaching out his thin hand to find thine. Touch him, dear Savior, with thy loving, warm clasp. Lift him as he passes the cold river, that his feet be not chilled by the water of death; take him home in thine own good time. Comfort and cherish him till that good time comes. Show him thyself as he lies here, and let

him see thee and know thee more and more as his
loving Saviour."

After a moment's pause, he said, "Now dear is
there anything you would like? Would you like
a little canary in a cage to hear him sing in the
morning? Nurse, see that he has a canary to-mor-
row morning. Good-bye, my dear; you will see the
Savior perhaps before I shall."

Gough had heard Spurgeon preach on multiple occasions,
"holding by his power sixty-five hundred persons in a breathless
interest." Gough knew Spurgeon as an international celebrity, "a
great man universally esteemed and beloved." But on that day,
Gough saw something different, something greater. As Spurgeon
prayed by a dying orphan's bedside, "he was to me a greater and
grander man than when swaying the mighty multitude at his will."[1]

Spurgeon's ministry as a pastor centered around his local
church. At the heart of his ministry was the preaching of the Word
for the edification of the saints and the conversion of the lost. Much
of his time was given to doing the work of a pastor—leading the
elders, chairing church meetings, conducting membership interviews, providing pastoral care, and much more. But beyond a concern for the church, Spurgeon wanted to model for his people an
engagement in the world around him. His confidence in the gospel overflowed in activism that extended to London and beyond.
Spurgeon used his influence and opportunities to establish institutions like the Stockwell Orphanages and the Colportage Association
that sought to care for the poor and reach the lost.

---

[1] John B. Gough, *Sunlight and Shadows or Gleanings from my Life Work.
Comprising Personal Experiences and Opinions, Anecdotes, Incidents, and
Reminiscences, Gathered from Thirty-Seven Years' Experience on the Platform
and Among the People at Home and Abroad* (Hartford, CT: A.D. Worthington and
Company, 1881), 406–8.

In doing so, Spurgeon was simply being a Christian. As the greatest preacher of the nineteenth century, unique opportunities were presented to him, but he simply sought to be faithful. Not every Christian is expected to open an orphanage or establish a college. But every Christian should be faithful in the opportunities they have. Spurgeon expected this of every member of his church. He envisioned a working church, where every member served and worked for Christ. In his own tireless labors, he did not provide a proxy for the church to admire but a model for the church to follow.

There was much about the Metropolitan Tabernacle that was impressive—the large crowds, the magnificent building, their famous pastor. But what Gough observed in Spurgeon could also be applied to the congregation. What made the preaching of the gospel even more attractive to the unbelieving in London was the sacrificial love and service of the church members. As they cared for the poor, visited the sick, and befriended the stranger, the work of the Metropolitan Tabernacle upheld and adorned the preaching of the gospel.

This chapter will explore Spurgeon's vision for a working church. He rejected any professionalized view of Christian ministry. Instead, he taught his people that the work of the church was to be accomplished by the members of the church. This included both the care of the church itself and the ministry of the church to the world.

Obstacles to a Working Church

When it came to the work of the church, Spurgeon saw many problems and challenges. Perhaps the greatest issue was an overall passivity within the church. There were many people who attended church, listened to sermons, had their name on membership rolls, and even gave financially. These people could talk all day about the ministries of their churches and pastor. But when it came to actual service, they had nothing to show for it.[2] Spurgeon believed that in any given church, only one-sixth of the congregation did the work of the church. The remaining simply took credit and looked on passively.

Another barrier to a working church was the myth of the lay-clergy divide. For many, this justified their passivity. They believed that ministry work should be left to the professionals. This was prominent in the Church of England that emphasized a formally ordained and educated ministry. In their rituals, clerical garments, and other traditions, they promoted a separation between ministers and their people. So long as the Church of England continued holding on to the lay-clergy divide, Spurgeon believed they would remain ineffective. "However evangelical the Church of England may become, it will never be able to compete with Dissenting churches either in piety or usefulness until it gives due honour and scope to what it has been pleased to call lay agency."[3]

This problem was not limited to the Church of England. He saw the same temptation toward a professionalization of the ministry within Dissenting churches, including his own Baptist denomination. Such a view would prove disastrous for the ministry of those churches.

---

[2] "You go to see them, and you say, 'Well, what is your church doing?' 'Well, we bless God, we are doing a great deal; we have a Sabbath-school, with so many children; our minister preaches so many times, and so many members have been added to the churches. The sick are visited; the poor are relieved.' And you stop them, and say, 'Well, friend, I am glad to hear that you are doing so much; but which work is it that you take? Do you teach in the Sabbath school?' 'No.' 'Do you preach in the street?' 'No.' 'Do you visit the sick?' 'No.' 'Do you assist in the discipline of the church?' 'No.' 'Do you contribute to the poor?' 'No.' 'Yet I thought you said you were doing so much. Stand out, sir, if you please, you are doing nothing at all.'" *NPSP* 5:205.

[3] *S&T* 1866:428.

Some seem to think that this work devolves upon ministers only, or upon them and their brethren in office, their deacons and elders, but that it is to extend no further. We hear much, about "lay agency" nowadays, but we know nothing of any distinction between "clergy" and "laity" in this matter. All God's people are God's *kleros*, God's clergy. Or if there be any laity, any common people, all God's people are the laity, "a peculiar people, zealous of good works." Nothing has been more disastrous to the cause of Christianity than the leaving of the service of Christ to comparatively few of his professed followers. We shall never see the world turned upside down as it was in apostolic times until we get back to the apostolic practice, and all the saints are filled with the Holy Ghost, and speak for Christ as the Spirit gives them utterance.[4]

Therefore, Spurgeon refused to take on any titles or accept any honorary degrees. Upon his arrival in London, his deacons wanted him to be ordained and to take on the title of "Reverend." But he understood that these extra-biblical practices separated him from his people. For most of his ministry, Spurgeon was simply called "Pastor" or "Mr. Spurgeon." To him, his labors were no different than the labors of all faithful Christians, and he wanted his people to know that.

The nineteenth century also saw the growth of societies and other parachurch institutions. In providing a way for individuals and churches to cooperate, many Christians saw these societies as a modern and efficient way forward in all kinds of evangelistic, educational, and charitable causes. The problem was, however, that these

---

[4] *MTP* 56:459.

efforts were disconnected from the local church. For example, in the case of parachurch missionary societies, Spurgeon observed,

> To become a member of a missionary society, you
> have only to subscribe to it. If you were a very infi-
> del and subscribed, you would become a member.
> Nothing whatever is required of you but that you
> should simply give a money qualification and you
> become a member of that society. We have been
> wondering why our societies have not greater suc-
> cess. I believe the reason is because there is not
> a single word in the Book of God about anything
> of the kind. The Church of God is the pillar and
> ground of the truth, not a society! The Church of
> God never ought to have delegated to any society
> whatever, a work which it behooved her to have
> done herself.[5]

Spurgeon here identifies at least two problems with these parachurch ministries. First, there was no accountability for their members. Any doctrinal or moral standard tended to be minimal and nominal, and membership could be purchased simply with a qualifying donation. With such a pragmatic basis, Christians should not expect the work to be blessed by God. Second, in creating these societies, Christians neglected the unique role of the church. The church is "the pillar and ground of the truth." Rather than societies supporting the work of the church, Spurgeon observed churches that were outsourcing their work to societies. Such an arrangement would ultimately fail because this was not God's design.

Against such views, Spurgeon encouraged pastors to teach their people about the importance of connecting their service to

---

[5] *MTP* 7:363.

the church. "Christian labours, disconnected from the church, are like sowing and reaping without having any barn in which to store the fruits of the harvest; they are useful, but incomplete."[6]

A Right Understanding of Christian Ministry

If those are wrong approaches to pursuing Christian ministry, how can a pastor rightly promote a working church? Most importantly, Spurgeon believed there needed to be a biblical understanding of the gospel. It was only by the truth of the gospel that people were transformed to deny themselves and serve others. Therefore, the preaching of the Word stood at the heart of the church's ministry. Without the gospel, people would remain stuck in their passivity and self-deception.

But the gospel does not offer grace at a price. In his preaching, Spurgeon exulted in the freeness of God's grace through Christ. For those who expected their good works to commend themselves to God, Spurgeon was clear: Salvation was to be received freely by faith apart from works. The right way to promote a working church is not by legalism.

Rather, Spurgeon believed that true believers are transformed under the preaching of the gospel. Those who are saved are born again by the Holy Spirit. True conversion always produces the fruit of the Spirit in the Christian. This is how Christians are empowered to obey God and love their neighbors: they first come to believe in the Savior who loved them and gave His life for them.

But in addition to the gospel, Spurgeon did not shy away from preaching the imperatives of Scripture, even to his Christian congregation. He made it clear that such obedience was the fruit of the gospel. Christians needed to hear these imperatives because

---

[6] *AARM* 109.

through them, God brought about repentance and sanctification. Though some condemned such preaching "as containing very little gospel and too much about good works," Spurgeon saw this kind of preaching modeled by Jesus.

> Let it never be forgotten that what the law demands of us the gospel really produces in us. The law tells us what we ought to be, and it is one object of the gospel to raise us to that condition. Hence our Savior's teaching, though it be eminently practical, is always evangelical; even in expounding the law he has always a gospel design. Two ends are served by his setting up a high standard of duty; on the one he slays the self-righteousness which claims to have kept the law by making men feel the impossibility of salvation by their own works; and, on the other hand, he calls believers away from all content with the mere decencies of life and the routine of outward religion, and stimulates them to seek after the highest degree of holiness–indeed, after that excellence of character which only his grace can give.[7]

Along with preaching the gospel, Spurgeon believed and taught that the church should practice accountability. Even as the church affirmed the Christian's initial profession of faith through baptism, it continued to affirm that profession through the Lord's Supper. Simply put, there was a relationship of accountability that each member had with the church. The church was responsible for

---

[7] *MTP* 23:350.

warning those who ignored the commands of Christ and deceived themselves with an inactive faith.[8]

To my knowledge, the Metropolitan Tabernacle never disciplined a member for inactivity. But Spurgeon certainly thought about it! He admired the example of Johann Oncken, the German Baptist church planter, who made it a rule to ask every incoming member, "What are you going to do for Christ?" and wrote down the answer. If the member ceased to serve "it was a matter for church discipline, for he was an idle professor, and could not be allowed to remain in the church like a drone in a hive of working bees."[9] Though he never pursued discipline for inactivity, Spurgeon understood that the church should hold people accountable. That included challenging them to live out their faith in service.

The Effects of a Working Church

Through such teaching, the Metropolitan Tabernacle became an engine of Christian ministry, and unbelieving London took notice. Many unbelievers would have had no interest in the Tabernacle's celebrity pastor or his books or sermons. They might have even been annoyed by the noise and traffic leading to the church every Sunday. But as they observed the members loving and caring for one another, as they saw them engaging in friendship with their neighbors and in service to the poor, sick, and lonely, they noticed something different about the church. And many of them decided to give these Christians a hearing. The working church created a platform for the gospel.

---

[8] "Oh, if I have one idle member in the church, who talks of loving Christ, but does nothing for him, I would look that member in the face if I knew which one it was, and I would say that faith without works is dead, that the love which does not show itself in practical piety is a pretended love, a painted flame, and not the gift of heaven!" *MTP* 48:310.

[9] *GFW* 44.

Brethren, you may, if you will, dignify your minister by the name of bishop, you may give to your deacons and elders grand official titles, you may call your place of worship a cathedral, you may worship if you will with all the grandeur of pompous ceremonial and the adornments of music and incense and the like, but you shall have only the semblance of power over human minds unless you have something more than these. But if you have a church, no matter by what name it is called, that is devout, that is holy, that is living unto God, that does good in its neighborhood, that by the lives of its members spreads holiness and righteousness; in a word, if you have a church that is really making the world whole in the name of Jesus, you shall in the long run find that even the most carnal and thoughtless will say, "The church which is doing this good is worthy of respect, therefore let us hear what it has to say." Living usefulness will not screen us from persecution, but it will save us from contempt. A holy church goes with authority to the world in the name of Jesus Christ its Lord, and this force the Holy Spirit uses to bring human hearts into subjection to the truth.[10]

Inwardly, Spurgeon's emphasis on a working church had the effect of guarding the church from all kinds of distractions. He observed that in many churches, the reason why prayer was declining and worldly amusements increasing was because there was no work for the people to do and no urgency in their prayers. Once idleness comes in the church, people begin to look for other things

---

[10] *MTP* 25:348.

to occupy themselves. "But the man who is all aglow with love to Jesus finds little need for amusement."[11]

In this dynamic, there is something of a gospel feedback loop in a working church. As the preaching of the gospel goes out, the church is empowered to serve Christ. And as the church serves Christ in evangelism and ministry, the priority of the gospel is preserved and upheld. Spurgeon refused to let his congregation be passive in hearing the gospel. He called them to live out their faith in service to others.

A Working Church: Serving the Church

The first part of a working church was to care for the church itself. Apart from a faithful and holy church, the congregation shouldn't expect God to work through them in the world. In joining the church, every member committed themselves to doing their part to seeing the church prosper spiritually.

> Some such vow we made, too, when we united ourselves to the church of God. There was an understood compact between us and the church, that we would serve it, that we would seek to honor Christ by holy living, increase the church by propagating the faith, seek its unity, its comfort, by our own love and sympathy with the members. We had no right to join with the church if we did not mean to

---

[11] "He has no time for trifling. He is in dead earnest to save souls, and establish the truth, and enlarge the kingdom of his Lord. There has always been some pressing claim for the cause of God upon me; and, that settled, there has been another, and another, and another, and the scramble has been to find opportunity to do the work that must be done, and hence I have not had the time for gadding abroad after frivolities. Oh, to get a working church!" *GFW* 44.

give ourselves up to it, under Christ, to aid in its
prosperity and increase.[12]

Of course, the first part of seeing church prosperity was to care
for one's own walk with Christ. As members of the church, they now
represented the church. Therefore, "if you join a Christian Church,
take heed how you live, for your actions may become doubly
watched, and will be doubly sinful if you fall into inconsistency."[13]
It was the responsibility of every member to conduct themselves
with holiness in every dealing.

Each member was also called to faithful "attendance upon the
means of grace," not only on Sundays, but also during weeknights.
Perhaps the most basic ministry of every member was the ministry of attendance. Spurgeon particularly emphasized Monday-night
prayer meetings because he knew that the work of the church was
powerless apart from the work of God. "Any hypocrite comes on
a Sunday, but they do not, to my knowledge, all of them come on
Monday to the prayer-meeting."[14] Exceptions were granted for those
who could not gather because of distance or work, but those people
should still devote themselves to praying for the church. "If you
cannot come to the prayer-meetings—and many of you, I know,
cannot, and I do not speak to you, blaming you—do pray in the
family, do pray in the closet for us. Do not let us become poor in
prayer." Spurgeon believed prayer was more vital for the church
than the financial giving of the people. Not every member could
give to the church, but every member was responsible to pray for
her. "It is a bad thing to become poor in money . . . but we can do
without money better than we can do without prayer. . . . The very

---

[12] *MTP* 17:669.
[13] *MTP* 60:293.
[14] *MTP* 60:294.

least thing that a church member can do is to plead with God that the blessing may descend."[15]

Beyond these basic expectations, what did service at the Metropolitan Tabernacle look like? As was mentioned, members were responsible for supporting the work of the church financially. One way this was accomplished was through the common practice of seat rents. Members paid a regular fee to occupy a rented seat and those without a seat rent could occupy the free seats. These fees were typically used for paying the pastor's salary. Other church expenses would be covered by additional collections. Prior to Spurgeon's arrival, the seat rents hardly paid for church expenses and the deacons would have to send around the collection hat multiple times at the end of the year to balance the budget. But with his coming, the seat rents were quickly filled, and the church budget grew. Spurgeon's agreement with his deacons from the beginning was that whatever the seat rents produced would be his. But as those funds grew, Spurgeon refused to keep all the rents to himself. Rather, he put an end to any additional collections and began paying for the expenses of the church out of the seat rents.[16]

In addition to seat rents, members could give financially to the many ministries and institutions connected with the church through subscriptions (a pledge for regular giving) and one-time gifts tied with a particular cause. From the orphanages to the Pastors' College, to the almshouses, to new church plants, and much more, there was never a shortage of financial needs. Spurgeon sought to model generosity as most of his royalties from books and sermons were given to these various ministries. Some estimate that Spurgeon gave away the modern equivalent of hundreds of millions of dollars.[17]

---

[15] *MTP* 14:35.
[16] *Autobiography* 2:123
[17] *LS* 4:4.

As financial pressures grew, Spurgeon was aware of the temptation to compromise the purity of the church. After all, there was always more work to be done and new opportunities for the gospel. If the church grew, then the budget (and subsequently, the ministries of the church) would also grow. So why be so rigorous about church membership? Of course, Spurgeon was glad for the budget to grow, but not at the expense of regenerate church membership.

> If we could tomorrow bring into the Church a sufficient number of ungodly but moral men to double our numbers, to double our subscriptions, to double our places of worship, to enable us to double the number of our missionaries, we should by succumbing to the temptation procure a curse instead of a blessing. In our purity, and in our purity alone we stand.[18]

While Spurgeon was glad for those outside the church to give to the work, the primary responsibility for the church's financial support lay with the members of the church.

But giving financially would not be the limit of a member's church involvement. Spurgeon rebuked the common attitude that said, "When I pay my seat rent, I have done all I intend to do." Such an attitude gave no evidence of love for Christ. Beyond financial support, members had a vital role to play in the spiritual and material care of the church. Before they served those outside the church, the members were to care for the church itself.[19]

---

[18] *NPSP* 6:222.

[19] "Another duty of all church members is to aid and comfort one another. . . . You must comfort those that mourn, help those who are poor, and, in general, we ought to watch for each other's interests, seeing that in the church we are all members of one family. You are to "do good unto all men, especially unto such as are of the household of faith." Let your crumbs be given to the sparrows out of

There were many ministry opportunities inside the church. The elders sought to create a church culture where members took an interest in one another and engaged each other spiritually and with practical care. This could happen in multiple ways: individual relationships, Bible studies, service opportunities, smaller prayer meetings, and more. By participating in these ministries and engaging one another in them, members contributed to the spiritual growth of the whole church.

Spurgeon also emphasized ministry to both children and youth. He believed that the members of the church should provide "everything spiritual in the education of its members," including their families. This means that from the time an infant is born to becoming a member of the church, they should be ready to be received into "the infant-school" so that the family would not need to "go away from that church for any Christian privilege." Some parachurch organizations had begun to establish children's ministries disconnected from local churches, but Spurgeon believed that they had the negative effect of raising kids outside the church. Far better was for the church to take responsibility for these ministries. "I think that every church should have its own Sabbath-school, and that the pastor should be president of it, the elders should be the managers, and, as much as possible, the teachers should be members of that church."[20] At the Tabernacle, the emphasis of these schools was evangelistic and they often met on Sunday afternoons, between the morning and evening services. In 1869, the church reported 1,077 children in Sunday school classes, with 96 teachers.

Of course, as children grew and entered their teenage years, the Sunday-school format was no longer be fitting. Still, the church

---

doors, but let your brethren and your sisters have the most and best of what you can give. This is the plain duty of every Christian." *MTP* 60:294.

[20] C. H. Spurgeon, *Speeches by C. H. Spurgeon at Home and Abroad* (London: Passmore & Alabaster, 1878), 63.

sought to engage the youth. This happened primarily through smaller classes of youth.

> We have at the Tabernacle . . . one class conducted
> by one of the elders for the sons of the elders
> and deacons themselves; and during this year—
> blessed be God for it—while we had a large addi-
> tion of members at the beginning of the year, we
> had one or more from every deacon's family, who
> made a fair and good profession, giving every sign
> of genuine conversion, as far as we could judge.
> Thus we have classes for the officers' children,
> and for those who are sometimes called the upper
> classes. There must be two or three lads' classes,
> and let the teacher be a good, genial soul, who
> laughs more often than he cries, for boys don't
> like a miserable teacher; more flies are caught by
> honey than by vinegar. With a good, cheerful man
> to manage a young men's class, it may be made
> useful in many ways. Under suitable oversight,
> youths' prayer-meetings will do good service.[21]

In organizing these small groups, the church took advantage of any existing connections among the youth (for example, sons of elders or deacons). To lead them, the church found cheerful, winsome teachers, who knew how to relate to the youth, and appointed them over the groups. These groups likely met together regularly for spiritual edification, prayer, and friendship. There might have been larger meetings of the youth on occasion, but throughout the year, the primary youth ministry seems to have been in small groups.

---

[21] Spurgeon, *Speeches*, 63–64.

For those who had more theological interest, there was "a sort of catechetical seminary connected with our church," where they led attenders through the Westminster Shorter Catechism with Proofs. Once again, Spurgeon focused on keeping youth engaged. Rather than requesting simple memorization, the teacher explained it "with numerous illustrations" and anecdotes. Spurgeon believed that there was no "better summary of Scripture doctrine" than the Shorter Catechism, though he did have to make "a slight alteration in regard to baptism."[22]

As was the custom, classes were usually separated by sex. It was natural for classes to develop among the boys and men of the church, as there were more male teachers. But Spurgeon insisted that "female agency must not be forgotten." The church also had numerous women's prayer meetings and Bible classes, the most famous one led by Mrs. Lavinia Bartlett. Speaking in 1866, Spurgeon gave this description of her fruitful ministry,

> We have a class, in connection with the church, that is presided over by a sister, such a woman as I have scarcely ever met with, who has about eight hundred females under her charge. She throws herself thoroughly into the work; and last year that class yielded more than a hundred members to our church; to our College funds also they contributed about £200.[23]

Over the course of her ministry, more than 1,000 women joined the membership of the Tabernacle because of her evangelistic efforts. With a regular attendance of 700 to 800 women, Mrs.

---

[22] Spurgeon, *Speeches,* 64.
[23] Spurgeon, *Speeches*, 65.

Bartlett's class became "the largest adult class in the world."[24] These classes provided not only biblical teaching but spiritual relationships and friendships, as members were able to interact with one another outside of church gatherings.

A Working Church: Ministry Outside the Church

In 1884, the congregation celebrated Spurgeon's fiftieth birthday with a meeting to honor his ministry among them. During that meeting one of the deacons read a partial list of sixty-six institutions connected with the Metropolitan Tabernacle:

> The Almshouses; the Pastors' College; the Pastors' College Society of Evangelists; the Stockwell Orphanage; the Colportage Association; Mrs. Spurgeon's Book Fund, and Pastors' Aid Fund; the Pastors' College Evening Classes; the Evangelists Association; the Country Mission; the Ladies' Benevolent Society; the Ladies' Maternal Society; the Poor Ministers' Clothing Society; the Loan Tract Society; Spurgeon's Sermons' Tract Society; the Evangelists' Training Class; the Orphanage Working Meeting; the Colportage Working Meeting; the Flower Mission; the Gospel Temperance Society; the Band of Hope; the United Christian Brothers' Benefit Society; the Christian Sisters' Benefit Society; the Young Christians' Association; the Mission to Foreign Seamen; the Mission to Policemen; the Coffee-House Mission;

---

[24] Edward H. Bartlett, *Mrs. Bartlett and Her Class at the Metropolitan Tabernacle: A Biography by Her Son* (Cannon Beach, OR: Move to Assurance, 2018), 53–54.

The Metropolitan Tabernacle Sunday School; Mr. Wigney's Bible Class; Mr. Hoyland's Bible Class; Miss Swain's Bible Class; Miss Hobbs's Bible Class; Miss Hooper's Bible Class; Mr. Bowker's Bible Class for Adults of both Sexes; Mr. Dunn's Bible Class for Men; Mrs. Allison's Bible Class for Young Women; Mrs. Bartlett's Bible Class for Young Women; Golden Lane and Hoxton Mission (Mr. Orsman's); Ebury Mission and Schools, Pimlico; Green Walk Mission and Schools, Haddon Hall; Richmond Street Mission and Schools; Flint Street Mission and Schools; North Street, Kennington, Mission, and Schools; Little George Street Mission, Bermondsey; Snow's Fields Mission, Bermondsey; the Almhouses Missions; the Almshouses Sunday Schools; the Almshouses Day Schools; the Townsend Street Mission; the Townley Street Mission; the Deacon Street Mission; the Blenheim Grove Mission, Peckham; the Surrey Gardens Mission; the Vinegar Yard Mission, Old Street; the Horse Shoe Wharf Mission and Schools; the Upper Ground Street Mission; the Thomas Street Mission, Horselydown; the Boundary Row Sunday School, Camberwell; the Great Hunter Street Sunday School, Dover Road; the Carter Street Sunday School, Walworth; the Pleasant Row Sunday Schools, Kennington; the Westmoreland Road Sunday Schools, Walworth; the Lansdowne Place Sunday School; Miss Emery's Banner Class, Brandon Street; Miss Miller's Mothers' Meeting;

Miss Ivimey's Mothers' Meeting; Miss Francies
Mothers' Meeting.[25]

A few observations can be made about this list. Nineteen of
these are Bible classes and other institutions geared toward church
members. But as seen with Mrs. Bartlett's class, these classes were
not limited to members. They were also open to non-Christians.
Members of the Tabernacle regularly invited friends and neighbors to these classes, and many were converted through them.
Additionally, twenty-nine of these institutions were evangelistic missions. From the Coffee-House Mission to the Mission to
Policemen, to the Flower Mission, to mission stations located in
different parts of London, the members of the church looked for
ways to share the gospel outside the church walls.

Many of these ministries also involved care for the poor. As
church members served immigrants, the poor blind, the Jewish
community, and other poor communities, there were always opportunities for charitable help. In reading the reports of these ministries, it's clear that acts of mercy were a large component of their
work. It's also clear that those who served always had an eye to
the gospel. Even if their service did not lead to evangelistic conversations right away, the hope was always that doors for the gospel
would be opened through their service.

Spurgeon himself founded a few of these institutions, namely
the Pastors' College, the Stockwell Orphanage, and the Colportage
Association. Understandably, these ministries get the most bio-
graphical attention when discussing external ministries. But what
is striking about the list above is that as important as these three
ministries were, they were only a small part of the church's work.

---

[25] C. H. Spurgeon, *The Metropolitan Tabernacle: Its History and Work*
(Pasadena, TX: Pilgrim Publications, 1990), 2:7–8.

One reason we don't hear about these other institutions is likely because Spurgeon didn't have a hand in creating them. Neither were they organized or planned by the elders. Rather, they grew up from the entrepreneurial efforts of members in the church. Members came together and sought to be fruitful for Christ with the opportunities they had.

Nonetheless, these ministries remained a ministry of the church. All who served in them were members of the Metropolitan Tabernacle. As these ministries grew, more members got involved and more became invested in them. They regularly gave reports at Monday night prayer meetings so that the church could pray for their work. At their annual meetings (usually a tea followed by a report on the past year and planning for the year ahead), at least one elder would be in attendance, if not Spurgeon himself. There were so many institutions that on any given weeknight, if the congregation was not gathering, there was probably an institution using the church building for their annual meeting.

Writing in 1865, about a decade after his arrival, Spurgeon provided this survey of the ministries of the Metropolitan Tabernacle.

> The Sunday-school at the Tabernacle numbers about 900 scholars and 75 teachers. Other Sunday schools, and ragged schools, are sustained and conducted in other districts, in connection with the Tabernacle. The College, at first, was sustained by the pastor only. As it rose in usefulness and promise, the assistance of others was cheerfully rendered. In 1861, it was adopted by the Church as one of its own institutions; and became united with it at the opening of the Metropolitan Tabernacle. The number of the students at the present time is 91. Apart from these, there are evening classes for young men for languages,

science, and elementary tuition; the attendants at which number on the whole about 230. Popular lectures, during the winter months are delivered on Friday evenings in the lecture-hall to students and the public in general. Many of the students are engaged in preaching on Sabbath days in the metropolis and its suburbs, and in distant parts of the country; others are employed in connection with an Evangelists' Association which has numerous preaching-stations in neglected districts, and sends forth a host of men to proclaim the gospel in the open air. This association is chiefly sustained by the students at the evening classes. There are numerous Bible classes in connection with the Tabernacle. One is held every Monday evening, after the prayer-meeting, at which Mr. Rogers presides. This class is for discussion on given topics, for the purpose of practice in extemporaneous speaking, as well as instruction in Biblical subjects. It is well attended by all classes, and is particularly beneficial as a test of the oratorical powers of those who are desirous of entering the College. Bible classes are conducted by Mr. Stiff, Mr. Hanks, and Mr. John Olney. All are efficient and well attended. A ladies' class, conducted by Mrs. Bartlett, is both the most numerous and most remarkable in its immediate results; it numbers nearly 700, and 63 have joined the Church from it during the past year. There is a Bible-society depot at the Tabernacle, at which Bibles are sold at cost-price. Here is a Tract Society in extensive operation. There is a Jews' Society which holds its meetings monthly. A Ladies' Benevolent Society, a Maternal Association, a Missionary Working and a Sunday School Working are also in full operation. A Fraternal Association has lately been established, with the view of promoting more union of heart and effort amongst pastors and Churches of the same denomination. Missionary work is not neglected. Two City Missionaries are sustained by the Church and people; two other missionaries on the Continent, in Germany; and considerable aid is given to foreign missions. We have here the rare instance of a Christian Church containing within itself all the varied appliances of Christian zeal in modern times. These have risen successively, and expanded, as the spontaneous and appropriate expression of that zeal.[26]

The Tabernacle was a working church! In one sense, Spurgeon's fingerprints are all over it, but in another sense, his part in the work is rather limited. In Sunday schools, pastoral training, Bible classes, benevolent ministries, evangelistic missions, missionary support, and much more, the congregation worked together for the advancement of the gospel. Rather than relegating ministerial work to their pastor, they joined him in that work and multiplied his efforts far beyond what he could have done. This is what a working church is all about.

Conclusion

There are all kinds of barriers and pitfalls to a working church today. Many approach the church as consumers rather than

---

[26] *S&T* 1865:174–75.

producers. Some Christians are active in service, but without a commitment to the church, their work remains separate from the church. For some churches, the emphasis is so much on the internal that they have neglected their community. For others, their emphasis on mercy ministry has blurred the importance of gospel proclamation.

So, before you can get a working church, there is much work to be done by pastors and church leaders. The preaching of the gospel must be central. There must also be teaching on what it means to be a church. There must be the accountability of meaningful membership. The pastors and deacons must model sacrificial service in their own lives. Prayer meetings must be revived. And the congregation must be empowered to serve in all kinds of surprising ways.

Give your people a vision for a working church and see the work of the church multiplied far beyond what you could do alone.

9

THE CHURCH AGGRESSIVE

PASTORAL TRAINING AND CHURCH PLANTING

"I Shall Preach Unless You Cut Off My Head!"

In the fall of 1854, two members of the New Park Street Chapel came to their pastor with a serious concern: T. W. Medhurst, who had recently joined the church, had taken to open-air preaching! As a former rope-maker, Medhurst had no formal education and had never preached before. But now, having been converted under Spurgeon's preaching, he was out on the street corner preaching about Christ. These church members were "shocked at his want of education." They feared that "disgrace would be brought upon the cause" of the church. After all, their new pastor was already notorious for his popular preaching style. The last thing they needed was for one of his converts to cause more trouble. They asked Spurgeon to put an end to his preaching.

Spurgeon agreed to meet with Medhurst. But the meeting didn't go quite as expected.

> Accordingly, I had a talk with the earnest young brother; and, while he did not deny that his English was imperfect, and that he might have made mistakes in other respects, yet he said, "I must preach, sir; and I shall preach unless you

cut off my head." I went to our friends, and told them what he had said, and they took it in all seriousness. "Oh!" they exclaimed, "you can't cut off Mr. Medhurst's head, so you must let him go on preaching." I quite agreed with them, and I added, "As our young brother is evidently bent on serving the Lord with all his might, I must do what I can to get him an education that will fit him for the ministry."[1]

And so began Spurgeon's pastoral training.

As he began to invest in Medhurst's training, Spurgeon believed that this was the beginning of a greater work. Writing to him in 1855, Spurgeon confessed, "I have been thinking that, when you are gone out into the vineyard, I must find another to be my dearly-beloved Timothy, just as you are." Over time, his efforts would grow into the first institution connected with the church, the Pastors' College. This institution was the nearest to Spurgeon's heart, and he poured his heart and soul into it. But the Pastors' College was more than just a college. It was the engine behind the church planting and missionary efforts of the Metropolitan Tabernacle.

Each year, the college provided a report on the progress of their work and by 1890, they reported 828 graduates of the college since its founding, with 607 of them serving as "Pastors, Missionaries, and Evangelists." The annual report provided updates on ministries throughout Great Britain, the United States (including Missouri, Kansas, Ohio, Southern California, and New York), the Middle East, Africa, Australia, New Zealand, India, and Canada.[2] Spurgeon's pastoral ministry had a tremendous impact throughout the world. However, through the Pastor's College, Spurgeon's impact was

---

[1] *Autobiography* 2:150–51.
[2] *S&T* 1890:311–51.

truly incalculable, as it extended beyond the Tabernacle and past his lifetime, to hundreds of churches all over the world.

From the humble beginnings of the Pastors' College, Spurgeon could have never envisioned the institution having such an impact. But his aim was not any particular outcome. Rather, Spurgeon understood that pastoral training was part of the pastor's job description. Just as Paul commanded Timothy to raise up other preachers and teachers (2 Tim. 2:2), so "one minister brings another to Christ, and then charges that other to train other preachers and teachers to carry on the blessed work of evangelization."[3] Even though he had been pastoring in London for only a few months and there was so much to do, when the opportunity arose, Spurgeon devoted himself to training future pastors. Eventually, this training would become the work of not only the pastor, but the entire church.

In this chapter, we will look at the story of the Pastors' College and Spurgeon's commitment to pastoral training. We will also see how that commitment opened doors for church planting and missionary efforts. Through these efforts, Spurgeon multiplied not only himself through these pastors, but he multiplied his church through the churches they went on to lead.

Raising Up Preachers

On August 5, 1855, Spurgeon preached a sermon on 1 Corinthians 9:16 entitled "Preach the Gospel." His congregation was growing rapidly and there were nearly 2,000 coming to hear him. Many were converted and were growing under the preaching of the Word. But he was not content with just a large attendance. He wanted to raise up preachers of the gospel.

---

[3] *MTP* 57:514.

As one who began preaching at the age of sixteen, Spurgeon knew what it was like to be "checked" by older ministers. Certainly, Spurgeon believed that there was a place for wise counsel and instruction. He disapproved of the practice among Scotch Baptists, who had "no regular minister . . . but every man preaches who likes to get up and speak." Often, in those settings, those "who have little to say will often keep on the longest." Reflecting Paul's instructions, Spurgeon believed that the gathering of the church should be guided by the goal of edification. Therefore, as the one entrusted with the pulpit, he was very careful with whom he allowed to preach. Only those who were equipped to preach publicly should occupy the pulpit at the Tabernacle.

At the same time, Spurgeon did not want to "check" any young man's desire to preach. Rather, he encouraged the young men in his church to try their hand at preaching. There were all kinds of institutions and ministries in the church that could provide eager members with opportunities to test out their gifts.[4] And if there was anything he could do to assist them, he was ready to help.

As we've seen, Spurgeon took very seriously the call to ministry. There were many who came to him for pastoral training that he turned away because he could not discern any evidence of a divine call. At the same time, Spurgeon believed that Christian ministry was not only reserved for those with professional training. Every

---

[4] "If there be any talent in the Church at Park Street, let it be developed. If there be any preachers in my congregation let them preach. Many ministers make it a point to check young men in this respect. There is my hand, such as it is, to help any one of you if you think you can tell to sinners round what a dear Savior you have found. I would like to find scores of preachers among you. . . . Young man, go home and examine thyself, see what thy abilities are, and if thou findest that thou hast ability, then try in some poor humble room to tell to a dozen poor people what they must do to be saved. You need not aspire to become absolutely and solely dependent upon the ministry, but if it should please God, even desire it. He that desireth a bishopric desireth a good thing. At any rate seek in some way to be preaching the gospel of God." *NPSP* 1:268.

Christian, man or woman, was called to evangelism. Even more, every Christian man had the freedom to test his abilities and see if he might be gifted to preach. Rather than waiting "till they are invited to a chapel, or have prepared a fine essay, or have secured an intelligent audience," Spurgeon encouraged the men of his church to seek opportunities to teach Sunday school, give away tracts, serve as lay preachers in villages and hamlets, open mission stations, and more.[5] While holding up a high view of the pastorate, Spurgeon encouraged young men to examine themselves and ask, "Why shouldn't I begin preaching now?" For many of them, it was this step of obedience that led to pursuing pastoral training.[6]

As the young men of the congregation ventured out to preach, Spurgeon involved the congregation. They prayed for them in their prayer meetings. They rejoiced when the fruit of their preaching was seen in the baptism and joining of new converts. Spurgeon urged his people to not only pray for their pastor, but that God would raise up more faithful pastors out of their midst.[7] One of their most important prayers was that the Lord would send out workers into the harvest.

The Start of the Pastors' College

It was in this context that T. W. Medhurst began preaching and was trained for pastoral ministry. As an apprenticed rope-maker, Medhurst had no chance of being admitted to any Baptist college. He also had no resources to pay for an education. He only had a proven ability to preach the gospel, imperfect as it was, and the

---

[5] *Autobiography* 1:202.

[6] "I have preached this sermon especially, because I want to commence a movement from this place which shall reach others. I want to find some in my church, if it be possible, who will preach the gospel. And mark you, if you have talent and power, woe is unto you if you preach not the gospel." *NPSP* 1:268.

[7] *S&T* 1875:249.

evidence of God's seal on his ministry through the conversion of sinners. In other words, Medhurst was just the kind of student Spurgeon wanted to train.

It is remarkable to imagine the challenges ahead of him. Most aspiring ministers today have at least a high school degree. Many have had some level of college education, or even a Bible or theological degree. But for Spurgeon, because of his commitment to train up those called by God to preach, he was willing to take any who showed evidence of that divine call, "whether they were poor and illiterate, or wealthy and educated."[8] In fact, Spurgeon welcomed those who came from the lower classes, because these were the kind of preachers who could connect with common men more effectively. At the same time, their lack of education meant that Spurgeon had to start at the very beginning when it came to their pastoral training.

This was Medhurst's situation. So, in July of 1855, Spurgeon made arrangements for him to reside with Rev. C. H. Hosken, pastor of the Baptist church in Crayford, and to receive elementary instruction at the Mill Road Collegiate School in Bexley Heath, Kent. Out of his own limited salary, Spurgeon provided the funds for Medhurst's tuition, books, and living expenses.

Spurgeon was also personally involved in the training. Once a week, Medhurst met with him for several hours to study theology under his direction. Spurgeon also mentored Medhurst in his preaching. As he sat under Spurgeon's preaching week after week, he naturally began imitating his mentor. On one occasion, Spurgeon filled in for Medhurst in his open-air preaching and afterwards, he overheard one of the regulars wish that the guest speaker "hadn't imitated our dear Mr. Medhurst so much." Like any

---

[8] *Autobiography* 2:149.

preacher, Medhurst would grow discouraged in his preaching, but Spurgeon provided guidance for him during those times.

> One day, with a very sad countenance, he said to me, "I have been preaching for three months, and I don't know of a single soul having been converted." Meaning to catch him by guile, and at the same time to teach him a lesson he would never forget, I asked, "Do you expect the Lord to save souls every time you open your mouth?" "Oh, no, sir!" he replied. "Then," I said, "that is just the reason why you have not had conversions: 'According to your faith be it unto you.'"[9]

By late 1856, Medhurst had so grown in his preaching that he received a unanimous call to serve as the pastor of the Baptist church at Kingston-on-Thames. Spurgeon was pleased with Medhurst's growth but wasn't quite ready to release him. Medhurst still needed more formal theological training. So, Spurgeon advised that he only accept the position temporarily for two years, while continuing his training. Then, the church could call Medhurst more permanently as their pastor. Spurgeon also arranged that the church should also pay for his ongoing training and for the expenses associated with his education up to that point (which Spurgeon had covered). When Spurgeon received the check, he promptly handed it to Medhurst, but Medhurst refused to accept it. So, instead, Spurgeon used it to take on another student, and the pastoral training grew.

By March 1857, Spurgeon had found a more permanent tutor in Rev. George Rogers, a Congregationalist minister who shared all of Spurgeon's theological convictions, save on baptism. One biographer describes that initial meeting between Spurgeon and Rogers:

---

[9] *Autobiography* 2:151.

A meeting with Mr. Rogers was arranged, and
Mr. George accompanied Mr. Spurgeon and Mr.
Medhurst. Neither could have anticipated the
results of that meeting. Mr. Spurgeon was greatly
impressed by the transparent sincerity and solid
learning of the one whom he afterwards said was
preordained of God to be the first principal of the
college.

In the little sitting-room they all knelt in prayer,
and there in an amateurish sort of way the Pastors'
College was ushered into life.[10]

Medhurst went to live with Rogers and later that year, a second
student, E. J. Silverton, was accepted into the program.

Funding the Work

When Spurgeon supported just one student, the cost was £50
per year, quite a large sum for a young pastor. That cost would vary
depending on the student, but Spurgeon committed to ensuring
that financial cost was no obstacle to helping young men with evident preaching gifts to be trained for ministry. Not surprisingly, as
the church grew, so did the number of aspiring young preachers.
Most of these were members of the New Park Street Chapel and
were actively involved in the life of the church. As more students
were accepted into the program, some of them lived with Rogers
or with officers and members of the church. They met in Rogers's
home for their classes, which soon grew cramped. And as some were
sent out, more applied. Before long, two students grew to eight, and
then to sixteen.

---

[10] J. C. Carlile, *C. H. Spurgeon* (Barbour and Company: Westwood, NJ, 1987),
170–71.

Between 1856 and 1861, Spurgeon covered all the expenses for the Pastors' College (tuition, books, living expenses) entirely by himself from the proceeds of the sale of his sermons and books in America. Those sales, combined with Susannah's frugality, allowed Spurgeon to spend anywhere between £1,600–1,800 per year on this work (the equivalent of about $300,000 today). Spurgeon would trust God for other massive financial undertakings, like the construction of the Metropolitan Tabernacle or the founding of the orphanage. All these required tremendous faith. But the growing and strengthening of that faith began in these early years, with the training of pastors. "Faith trembled when tried with the weight of the support of one man; but the Lord has strengthened her by exercise, so that she has rejoiced under the load when multiplied a hundred-fold."[11] But this faith did not grow without severe testing.

In January 1860, Spurgeon wrote a letter to the *Christian Watchman and Reflector*, a Baptist newspaper based out of Boston, on the topic of slavery. He served as a correspondent for the newspaper, as a way of keeping in touch with his American audience. Preaching in London, where slavery had already been abolished, Spurgeon did not feel a need to address the issue directly in his sermons. But with a growing American audience that was increasingly divided, Spurgeon made his position clear:

> I do from my inmost soul detest slavery anywhere and everywhere, and although I commune at the Lord's table with men of all creeds, yet with a slaveholder I have no fellowship of any sort or kind. Whenever one has called upon me, I have considered it my duty to express my detestation of his wickedness, and would as soon think of

---

[11] *Autobiography* 2:148.

receiving a murderer into my church, or into any
sort of friendship, as a manstealer.[12]

Response to this letter was swift. By the spring of 1860, his
sales in the American South plummeted. Southerners published
threats against him and held book burnings. Friends warned him
to not accept any speaking engagements in America or he might be
killed. As his sales dropped, the college funds also quickly dwindled.
Spurgeon continued paying for the training out of his own pocket
and was resolved to spend all that he had. He offered to sell his
horse and carriage, which were much needed for his frequent travel,
but Rogers would not hear of it and offered to bear the shortfall.
Whatever the arrangement, Spurgeon refused to go into debt. Once
everything was spent, Spurgeon would take that as a sign from God
that the work was over.

But the work did not end. In May 1861, with the support of his
deacons and elders, Spurgeon brought the matter to his congregation, and they took up a special offering for the Pastors' College. But
the congregation would do more than just take up an offering. Two
months later, the congregation would pass the following motion,

> Our Pastor having told the Church of his
> Institution for educating young ministers, and
> having informed them that several were now set-
> tled in country charges and laboring with great
> success, it was unanimously agreed,—That this
> Church rejoices very greatly in the labours of our
> Pastor in training young men for the ministry and
> desires that a record of his successful & laborious
> efforts should be entered in the church-books—
> Hitherto, this good work has been rather a private

---

[12] C. H. Spurgeon, "Spurgeon on Slavery," *The Christian Watchman and
Reflector,* January 26, 1860.

effort than one in which the Church has had a share, but the Church hereby adopts it as part of its own system of evangelical labours, promises its pecuniary aid, and its constant and earnest prayers.[13]

From that point on, the Pastors' College would be a ministry of their pastor *and* the church. The classes of the Pastors' College were moved to the basement of the newly constructed Metropolitan Tabernacle. Every week, an offering was taken for the work of the College. More importantly, now that the church owned it, the College became more public and prominent. People outside the church began giving to it, even as applicants increased. In those early years, there were many instances when the College was down to the last pound and an anonymous gift would arrive just in time to sustain it. But in 1865, Spurgeon's deacons and other friends began organizing annual dinners and other fundraisers to provide stability for the institution's future.

Church-Based Pastoral Training

But more than financially providing for the College, the church itself became an integral part of Spurgeon's pastoral training program. Many of the students at the Pastors' College began as members of the church. In addition to growing under the preaching, they became involved in Bible studies, discipleship, and various service opportunities. Those needing a basic education could attend evening classes at the church freely, without giving up their jobs. If they developed gifts in speaking, they were encouraged to pursue teaching and preaching opportunities. Before applying to the Pastors' College, Spurgeon required at least two years of lay

---

[13] *Autobiography* 3:125–26.

preaching and ministry experience in the church. Spurgeon cautioned those who aspired to ministry,

> Brethren, we have no right to thrust a brother into the ministry until he has first given evidence of his own conversion, and has also given proof not only of being a good average worker but something more. If he cannot labor in the church before he pretends to be a minister, he is good for nothing. If he cannot whilst he is a private member of the church perform all the duties of that position with zeal and energy, and if he is not evidently a consecrated man whilst he is a private Christian, certainly you do not feel the guidance of God's Holy Spirit to bid him enter the ministry.[14]

In addition to looking for evidence of conversion, proven ability to teach, and a track record of faithful service in the church, Spurgeon also brought in an additional requirement for every student: "a man must, during about two years, have been engaged in preaching, and must have had some seals to his ministry, before we could entertain his application."[15] What were these "seals to his ministry"? Nothing less than the supernatural work of God to bring sinners to salvation through the preaching of the Word. "There must be some measure of conversion-work in your irregular labors before you can believe that preaching is to be your life-work."[16] This requirement arose out of Spurgeon's conviction to train up preachers and pastors, not scholars. No tutor could make a student into

---

[14] *MTP* 12:412–13.
[15] *Autobiography* 2:148.
[16] *Lectures* 1:29.

a preacher, but they wanted to help "those whom God had already called to be such."[17]

Spurgeon turned down many applicants over the years. Some accused the Pastors' College of being a pastor factory, but Spurgeon denied ever being able to produce a minister. If anything, he thought himself to be a "parson-killer" for all the applicants he denied. It was a difficult task to turn down an eager applicant, but an important one for the good of churches.[18]

What was training at the Pastors' College like? Initially, it was a two-year program, but later it would grow to three. For their education, students engaged in courses on Greek, Hebrew, Latin, biblical studies, theology, history, classical literature, ethics and philosophy, English studies, rhetoric, logic, preaching, and more. Classes were divided by junior, middle, and senior levels. Courses were rigorous and disciplined, but also were marked by a collegial spirit. The theology of the College was robustly Calvinistic. And every subject was geared toward the pastorate, not the academy. A few students did go on to pursue careers in scholarship, but most graduates went on to be pastors and missionaries.

The favorite part of the week for all students was on Friday afternoons. After a long week of study and lectures, the students eagerly anticipated hearing from their President. But this was not a typical classroom lecture. First, Spurgeon would come with a stack of books chosen out of his own voracious reading. From these, he would read selections and recommend authors to his students.

---

[17] *Autobiography* 2:148.

[18] "It has often been a hard task for me to discourage a hopeful young brother who has applied for admission to the College. My heart has always leaned to the kindest side, but duty to the churches has compelled me to judge with severe discrimination. After hearing what the candidate has had to say, having read his testimonials and seen his replies to questions, when I have felt convinced that the Lord has not called him, I have been obliged to tell him so." *Autobiography* 3:143.

These books included works of theology, preaching, science, philosophy, poetry, and more. A former student writes,

> Week by week we were advised what books to buy. To many this advice has proved of almost priceless value . . . as theological students we were equally thankful to be introduced to Augustine, Owen, Baxter, Brooks, Charnock, Manton, Sibbes, and to a host of other illustrious names, whose writings embraced varied fields of literature and science.[19]

Then, Spurgeon would give a lecture on topics dealing "with every conceivable phase of life and experience that bore any relationship to the Christian ministry." Many of these lectures are published in the series *Lectures to My Students*, which, even to this day, are an excellent source of pastoral instruction. And yet,

> these in print give but a faint indication of the numerous subjects that at one time or another were the theme of his enchanting talk; talk charged with wit and humour, repartee and raillery, anecdote and illustration, mimicry and genuine bursts of oratory, and which filled many an hour with merriment, and sometimes with even boisterous abandon; yet with such merriment and abandon that a closing prayer which carried all spirits into the presence of the Eternal seemed the most harmonious and fitting ending to the afternoon's instruction and delight. The brightest and

---

[19] W. Williams, *Personal Reminiscences of Charles Haddon Spurgeon* (London: The Religious Tract Society, 1895), 146–48.

most stimulating memories of many a minister's life come from the Fridays of their college days.[20]

Beyond the classroom, the other major component of the training at the Pastors' College was its integration with the Metropolitan Tabernacle. This was, in many ways, what set the College apart from all other colleges.[21] As important as preaching was, the Pastors' College sought to train up *pastors*. The church, therefore, provided a context for pastoral training. Most students either joined the church or were already members of the church, and many lived with officers of the church or other prominent members. All students were immersed in the life of the church. James Spurgeon once wrote about this aspect of the instruction,

> We have, therefore, kept ever in mind the strong necessity of our young brethren taking part in all our prayer-meetings, occasionally attending our church meetings, constantly helping in our varied platform meetings, and watching in general all the departments of work . . . which encircle the Tabernacle as the centre of their influence and the mainspring of their order and power. . . . Special lectures are given on the points of church government and procedure, so that no man need be

---

[20] *Personal Reminiscences of Charles Haddon Spurgeon*, 146–48.

[21] "The relation of the College to a large and active Church, by which it is principally sustained, and which takes a lively interest in its welfare, is one special means of its prosperity. The intercourse of the Students with the Members of the Church contributes much to their social and their spiritual welfare. The officers of the Church cheer them by their kindness and aid them by their counsel. A familiarity with Church discipline is acquired, and with all the appliances by which a flourishing Church is sustained and enlarged, which is treasured up for future use, and supplies what has hitherto often proved to be a serious deficiency in a College education for the pastoral office." *S&T* 1866:197–98.

altogether at a loss how to act in the emergencies
of church discipline and care.[22]

Upon graduation from the Pastors' College, students would be
familiar not only with the biblical languages and Reformed theology, but also how to lead church meetings, investigate discipline
cases, relate to their deacons, and more. The training was both
theological and practical.

Beyond the classroom, the students also cherished their time
with their pastor. Spurgeon and Susannah often had students in
their home for dinner and fellowship. One moving account of
such a time was when the Spurgeons hosted T. L. Johnson, C. H.
Richardson, and their wives on the eve of their departure for Africa
to serve as missionaries. They were former slaves from America,
and the husbands had studied at the Pastors' College. Susannah
recounts, "A very pleasant and memorable time we spent together,
their Pastor encouraging them in the work to which they had
devoted themselves, and their love and sympathy overflowing to
him and to me—then very sick—in return." At one point, the discussion turned to their experience as slaves, and they shared about
the songs of hope they used to whisper in captivity, fearing their
masters might find them singing and punish them. Then Susannah
asked,

> "Will to me in you sing to me in whispers you sang
> then?" . . . and they very sweetly complied with my
> wish. . . . I shall never forget that painful hushing
> of their voices. There was not a dry eye in that little
> company when the song was ended; but we wiped
> our tears away, soon remembering that the cause
> for sorrow no longer existed. [They] are now free,

---

[22] *S&T* 1881:309.

noble educated men and women; they can sing and pray and preach as loudly and as long as they please, and are bound for the land of their fathers, with the intention of exercising these privileges to the full, and making known the Gospel of the Grace of God to their kindred according to the flesh. The Lord go forth with them and prosper them. The echoes of that singular song have lingered with me ever since, and many a time have they comforted my heart.[23]

From time to time, Spurgeon invited students to join him on his day off for a ride out to the country. These trips were always full of instructive conversations and rich memories for the students. At the start of every semester, students were also invited to spend the day at the Spurgeon home in Westwood, where they were able to explore the grounds, play lawn games, visit his study, and meet with Spurgeon. One large tree on the property, "The Question Oak," served as a gathering spot where students could sit and ask him any question at all. As Spurgeon was accessible to his congregation, even more so, he made himself accessible to his students.

Training at the Pastors' College included much more than just the classroom. It included the students' involvement in a vibrant and working church, where they actively used their gifts. It also included their life-on-life engagement with their pastor, as they watched him pastor the church. These three elements—theological, ecclesiological, and pastoral—served as the three-legged stool of the church-based training at the Pastors' College.

[23] Thomas L. Johnson, *Twenty-Eight Years a Slave: Or the Story of My Life in Three Continents* (Bournemouth: W. Mate & Sons, Ltd, Printers and Publishers, 1909), 106.

From Pastoral Training to Church Planting

As the reputation of the Pastors' College grew, Baptist churches needing a pastor began contacting Spurgeon, to ask if he might have a student he could recommend. In the first two decades of the school, the need was so great that many students received a pastoral call before they finished their two-year course of study. Spurgeon often advised against it, but in the end, he respected the congregational authority of each church. For a student eager to preach, it was hard to turn down the offer and many went against their president's wishes. Even so, these early graduates remained a part of the Pastors' College network and continued benefitting from the ongoing relationships.

Spurgeon's interactions with deacons looking for a pastor provided many memorable interactions. Too often, these deacons hoped for a pastor who could reproduce Spurgeon's success. On one occasion, a deacon wrote to Spurgeon asking if he had a student who could "fill the chapel." Spurgeon wrote back saying that he did not have one "big" enough, but if he were interested in a student who could fill the pulpit and preach the gospel faithfully, he would happily recommend someone. The deacon quickly responded to confirm that this is what he had meant. Spurgeon, with no small delight, recommended to him a Mr. Whale. Whale went on to be a fruitful minister in England and later in Australia.

As the London population grew during the second half of the nineteenth century, the dynamics of the city also changed. As pollution and overcrowding grew in the city, the upper and middle class began to move out to the suburbs. This created new challenges for churches. Preaching in 1859, Spurgeon recognized that the growing suburbs needed new churches. Many believers continued to attend city churches but would miss opportunities to evangelize their neighbors.[24] Rather than commuting into the city, Spurgeon believed that Christians needed to work together to plant new churches in the suburbs.

But very quickly, that dynamic would change. By 1861, Spurgeon noted a different trend,

> You know that in the City of London itself, there is now scarce a Dissenting place of worship. The reason for giving most of them up and moving them into the suburbs, is that all the respectable people live out of town, and of course, they are the people to look after. They will not stop in London, they will go out and take villas, and live in the suburbs; and therefore, the best thing is to take the endowment which belonged to the old chapel, and go and build a new chapel somewhere in the suburbs where it may be maintained.[25]

Now, it was city churches that needed support. Rather than planting new churches, wealthier members were transferring the endowments of city churches out to suburb churches, leaving the poorer members behind who could not afford to move out. As a result, many city churches were in serious decline as they lost their members and funding to the suburbs. Not being able to pay for their own pastor, many of them had to hire a city missionary. Even though they had a building and a handful of remaining members,

---

[24] "There needs to be in many of the suburbs of London fresh gospel churches springing up. I can point to many places in my own vicinity, seven or eight, nine or ten in a row, where there is a chapel needed. In each place there are believers living, who do not think about uniting to establish a fresh cause; but as long as their peculiar wants are satisfied, by journeying a long way off perhaps, they forget the hundreds and thousands who are pressing around them." *NPSP* 5:304.

[25] *MTP* 7:375.

Spurgeon saw that "the resurrection and salvation of an old church is often a more difficult task than to commence a new one."[26]

As Spurgeon observed the needs around him, he lamented, "Oh! there is much to be done, and very little time to do it in." But this is why the Pastors' College existed. From the very beginning, Spurgeon's plan "was not only to train students, but to found churches."[27] Both in planting brand new churches and in revitalizing old churches, graduates of the Pastors' College eagerly attempted this ground-breaking and difficult work. After all, their own pastor had done it at New Park Street, through the faithful preaching of the Word. Through his ministry, this dying church was revived. They too hoped that they might be a part of such a work in their lifetimes. Because of their efforts, hundreds of churches throughout London and beyond would be revitalized and established.

Church Planting Process

What was the church planting process out of the Metropolitan Tabernacle? First, one or two students would identify a location with little or no evangelical presence and establish a mission station, usually in a public hall or some rented building. There, the team would hold public services. Additionally, they also began evangelizing the community, distributing tracts, going door-to-door, visiting hospitals, and more. This was difficult work. There was no guaranteed timetable for how long until they saw their first converts. However, they had the encouragement of the other students and the prayers of the congregation sustaining them. Sometimes church members who lived in the area would also join the students in the work. Over time, many of these mission stations saw people converted.

---

[26] S&T 1878:263.
[27] S&T 1878:240.

Once they saw new converts, the next step was to bring them into membership at the Metropolitan Tabernacle. They typically went through the normal membership process. But on occasions where converts were coming from a long distance, accommodations were made, either in sending out elders for interviews or scheduling services at more convenient times.

Once there were enough members in the area to form a church, a formal letter was sent to the Metropolitan Tabernacle, recounting the work that God had done, expressing their desire to form a new church, and requesting to be dismissed from membership for that purpose. This letter would be read at a congregational meeting and voted on for approval. Elders were also appointed to help the new church constitute. At this point, the newly formed church would vote to call their pastor and other church officers and would celebrate the Lord's Supper together for the first time. In earlier years, the congregation at the Tabernacle would often send a parting gift of a communion service for the new churches.

Supporting the New Churches

Once a church was planted, that didn't mean it was fully self-sufficient from the very beginning. Spurgeon recognized that many of these churches and pastors still needed support. So, he sought to be generous in three ways. First, he was generous with his members. Spurgeon encouraged his members to join these church planting efforts, especially those who lived near those new churches. By attending a church nearer to their homes, this opened evangelistic opportunities for their neighbors. In giving of his members freely, he did not see this as working against his own church's growth. Rather, it contributed to it as God blessed their faith.[28]

---

[28] "We have never sought to hinder the uprising of other churches from our midst or in our neighborhood. It is with cheerfulness that we dismiss our twelves, our twenties, our fifties, to form other churches. We encourage our members to

Thus, every church plant was marked by a joyful congregational meeting when the members commissioned and prayed for those being sent out. In 1878, the church dismissed 75 members for the church plant at James Grove, Peckham. Spurgeon sent them with this blessing,

> You are such beloved and useful members that we should have been grieved to part with you under any other circumstances; but now we send you out as a father sends out his full-grown son to found another house, and to become himself the center of a family. We wish you every blessing. It is our joy to see our Lord's Kingdom increased; and, as we believe that your being gathered into it new church will tend to that grand design, we gladly part with you, wishing you the power and presence of the Lord henceforth and for ever.[29]

Spurgeon also modeled financial generosity. As the Pastors' College grew in prominence, he was sometimes able to raise more money than was needed for that year's expenses. But Spurgeon refused to create an endowment. He would not fund the school into the future when he had no guarantee of what it might teach.

> I am against all endowments for religion; it is better to spend the money for immediate needs. I am not even in favor of endowing my own College. Someone made me an offer, the other day, to found a scholarship in connection with it, but I declined it. Why should I gather money, which

---

leave us to found other churches; nay, we seek to persuade them to do it. We ask them to scatter throughout the land to become the goodly seed which God shall bless. I believe that so long as we do this we shall prosper." *MTP* 11:238.

[29] *Autobiography* 3:253–54.

> would remain after I am gone, to uphold teach-
> ing of which I might entirely disapprove? No! let
> each generation provide for its own wants. Let my
> successor, if I have one in the College, do as I have
> done, and secure the funds which he needs for his
> own teaching.[30]

Instead, Spurgeon decided that any excess funds would go to launching their graduates in the ministry. This could mean helping a smaller church pay for their pastor's salary, or assisting a church plant with building a new chapel, or even supplementing a new pastor's library.

Finally, Spurgeon supported these church planting efforts by forming a network of like-minded churches and pastors. As it grew, Spurgeon looked for ways to coordinate their efforts and encourage pastors in the trenches. In 1865, Spurgeon started a monthly magazine, *The Sword and the Trowel*, which provided a channel for his graduates to stay in touch and share about their work. He also began the Pastors' College Conference for all those currently and formerly connected to the Pastors' College to gather once a year at the Metropolitan Tabernacle for mutual encouragement and edification. Those meetings proved to be joyful and life-giving for weary and discouraged pastors, strengthening them in their labors to persevere.

As the years went on and College graduates were sent out, Spurgeon rejoiced to see the growth of a network of theologically robust, ecclesiologically like-minded churches. The fact that he was in London allowed his church to function as a kind of hub church, sending out pastors and churches to other parts of the region,

---

[30] *Autobiography* 4:240.

country, and even the world. In all of this, he saw the advancement of the gospel that we see in the New Testament.[31]

Conclusion

Pastoral training is just a part of the pastor's job. As a seminary professor, I am a big believer in the usefulness of seminaries. For those aspiring to pastoral ministry, a seminary can be a great help to churches in equipping students in the biblical languages, theology, church history, and much more. But the role of the seminary is a support role. Seminaries alone cannot produce pastors. Rather, they work best when they come alongside local church pastors and support them in pastoral training.

So, if you're a pastor or a church leader, consider and pray about how you might begin a pastoral training program in your church. It's okay to start small but be committed to the work. Over the years and decades, the total impact of this investment will be significant. The course of training doesn't have to be complicated. Allow aspiring young men to attend elders' meetings, to have opportunities to preach and get feedback, to study ecclesiology and pastoral ministry, to accompany the pastor in his work . . . in other words, immerse them in the life of a pastor.

Such a program will require the congregation's support. After all, it will take time from the pastor that would have otherwise been

---

[31] "The Christian Church was designed from the first to be aggressive. It was not intended to remain stationary at any period, but to advance onward until its boundaries became commensurate with those of the world. It was to spread from Jerusalem to all Judea, from Judea to Samaria, and from Samaria unto the uttermost part of the earth. It was not intended to radiate from one central point only; but to form numerous centers from which its influence might spread to the surrounding parts. In this way it was extended in its first and purest times. The plan upon which the apostles proceeded, and the great apostle in particular in his mission to the Gentiles, was to plant Churches in all the great cities and centers of influence in the known world." *S&T* 1865:174.

given to his members. Even as the pastor devotes himself to training these men, many of them will never join church staff. But as the church invests in these men, prays for them, and sends them out, they will rejoice to see that they are a part of the larger work of the gospel. Give your people a vision for the advancement of the church and start where you are.

10

CONCLUSION

THE FAITHFUL PASTOR
AND HIS CHURCH

As we have observed Spurgeon as a model of faithfulness, it might be easy to walk away thinking that his ministry was one continuous wave of success after another. The huge congregation, the published sermons, the Pastors' College, the ministries of the church, all these things dazzle our imagination and leave us with an impression of Spurgeon as being super-human. But that is certainly not how Spurgeon viewed himself. And the end of his ministry was marked more by heartache than by any triumphalism.

The Suffering Pastor

As we have seen, Spurgeon labored under a crushing load. The physical work of preaching multiple times a day, attending meetings, writing correspondence, producing books, editing sermons, traveling, and much more, would be enough to exhaust even the most energetic of pastors; not to mention the emotional burden of pastoring a congregation of thousands of members and giving oversight to dozens of institutions. There was also the ongoing financial pressure of maintaining the orphanage, providing for his students, and supporting the almshouses. At home, he had two growing boys to raise and an invalid wife to care for.

All those pressures would have been difficult for any healthy pastor to bear. But Spurgeon was not a healthy pastor. Within the first few years of his ministry, he fell seriously ill from overwork. As the years went on, this would become a pattern for him. He would work himself to the ground and then be forced to take a few weeks or months off to recover. As he grew older, debilitating ailments began to plague him. Gout, kidney stones, and smallpox afflicted him throughout his middle-age years.

Spurgeon also struggled emotionally. In 1856, at the Surrey Gardens Music Hall, Spurgeon preached before a crowd of more than 10,000 people. During the service, a troublemaker yelled, "Fire!" resulting in a stampede. Seven people died and many more were injured. While trying to restore order amid the chaos, Spurgeon fainted and had to be carried out. For the rest of his life, he felt the weight of that event. Though he recovered enough to return to ministry, he continued to struggle with seasons of discouragement and darkness throughout his life. Modern psychiatrists may very well diagnose Spurgeon with depression and PTSD.

The story of Spurgeon's sufferings is worth telling all by itself, but that is for another time. Suffice it to say, Spurgeon saw himself as a needy sufferer. He felt deeply his dependence on God for strength in his ministry and in the health of the church. And yet amid his weakness, Spurgeon rejoiced to see God faithfully answer his prayers and the prayers of his people.

The Heartbroken Pastor

As Spurgeon grew older, his health continued to suffer. But the hardest blow would come not from any physical ailment or depression, but from the Downgrade Controversy. In the summer of 1887, Spurgeon published articles in *The Sword and the Trowel* condemning the infiltration of liberal theology among Baptist and other Dissenting churches. While liberal theology used much of the same vocabulary as historic Christianity, Spurgeon recognized that they meant something very different by it. This was no Christianity at all.

> A new religion has been initiated, which is no more Christianity than chalk is cheese; and this religion, being destitute of moral honesty, palms itself off as the old faith with slight improvements, and on this plea usurps pulpits which were erected for gospel preaching. The Atonement is scouted, the inspiration of Scripture is derided, the Holy Spirit is degraded into an influence, the punishment of sin is turned into fiction, and the resurrection into a myth, and yet these enemies of our faith expect us to call them brethren, and maintain a confederacy with them![1]

Spurgeon had hoped these articles would spark change in the Baptist Union. But even as conversation among pastors increased around these issues, the leadership refused to do anything about it at the annual meeting. As a result, Spurgeon did the unthinkable: he withdrew from the Baptist Union in the fall of 1887. He would not remain in association with ministers who denied historic Christianity. This act set off a massive debate in the press and among the churches. Many of Spurgeon's allies, including former students, turned against him for his stand.

In January 1888, the Union Council would pass a vote of censure against Spurgeon, rebuking him publicly for his behavior. Later that spring, the Union would pass a theological declaration that supposedly vindicated it from Spurgeon's charges and affirmed

---

[1] *S&T* 1887:397.

its evangelical character. But this declaration did nothing to enforce the doctrinal convictions of the Union's members but only spoke to its historic beliefs. Spurgeon was especially heartbroken because his brother, James, had supported and voted for the declaration. According to Susannah, it was this conflict and the ensuing heartbreak that killed Spurgeon less than four years later.[2]

The Downgrade Controversy was the last painful episode of Spurgeon's life. One of the reasons why his books are housed in Kansas City is because toward the end of his life, he was seen as a theological dinosaur. After his death, when his books were put up for auction in the United Kingdom, none of the ministers over there were interested. One minister wrote to his friend warning him not to be "tricked in buying it." It consisted "largely of old Puritan commentaries, etc., which today are almost worthless. Spurgeon evidently was no scholar, and I fear he did not buy books that are worth much today."[3] Only in 1906 did the Missouri Baptists purchase Spurgeon's books. Spurgeon was still respected in his later years for all that he did, but it's evident that younger pastors around him were moving on to theologies that kept with the times.

The Faithful Pastor

As he watched pastors turn away from the gospel, as he watched publishers and colleges market the new theology, as he watched associations abandon doctrinal standards, Spurgeon became even more convinced of the truth that he had held from the beginning: the church is the pillar and ground of truth; not the pastor, or the denomination, but the *church*, that gathering of faithful men and women under the gospel, set apart from the world by baptism and

---

[2] *Autobiography* 4:255.
[3] "Letter from Burrage to Mullins" January 3, 1906, The Southern Baptist Theological Seminary Archives.

the Lord's Supper. It is the church that exists to protect and proclaim the gospel.

Therefore, the best thing that he could do amid the confusion of his day was to continue pastoring his church: to keep preaching faithful sermons, practicing meaningful membership, raising up elders and deacons, mobilizing his congregation, training up pastors, and planting gospel-preaching churches. Writing in the beginning of 1890, two years after the painful events of the Downgrade Controversy, Spurgeon reveals the heart of his apologetic strategy for the gospel:

> We, being assured of the gospel, go on to prove its working character. More than ever must we cause the light of the Word to shine forth. . . . If sinners are converted in great numbers, and the churches are maintained in purity, unity, and zeal, evangelical principles will be supplied with their best arguments. A ministry which, year by year, builds up a living church, and arms it with a complete array of evangelistic and benevolent institutions, will do more by way of apology for the gospel than the most learned pens, or the most labored orations.[4]

A living church is the best defense for the truth of the gospel. This was Spurgeon's conviction. And this is what he sought to live out to the very end.

---

[4] *S&T* 1890:3.

ACKNOWLEDGMENTS

This book exists only because of the generous contribution of so many others. I'm grateful for the team at B&H Publishing for making this book a reality. My research in Spurgeon began during my doctoral studies at Midwestern Baptist Theological Seminary, and I would like to thank Jason Allen for his leadership of the school and his vision for the Spurgeon Library. I'm also thankful for Jason Duesing for supervising my doctoral research and mentoring me in my transition to my new academic post. My research assistants—Quinn, Aaron, and Micah—also helped me in my research for this book. I would also like to thank the Metropolitan Tabernacle for their kind hospitality during my visit in 2017, and Hannah Wyncoll for her ongoing correspondence in answering my questions.

My interest in Spurgeon's pastoral ministry has been shaped by my membership in faithful local churches over the years. I'm thankful for Houston Chinese Church, where I heard the gospel and was baptized; for Mark Dever and Capitol Hill Baptist Church, where I was discipled to love and serve the church; for Michael Lawrence and Hinson Baptist Church, who patiently bore with me and taught me how to be a pastor; and for Wornall Road Baptist Church, where I currently have the privilege of worshiping and serving.

I'm thankful for my family who has supported me over the years in all my endeavors; for my parents, who sacrificed so much for their children and continue to model faithful service to Christ and His church; my kids, who have been a source of deep joy and healthy distraction amid the pressures of life; and my dear wife, who has supported me in all my endeavors. Thank you!

Finally, to my Lord and Savior Jesus Christ, the great Shepherd of the sheep, who loved the church and gave Himself up for her, to Him be all thanks and glory forever. Amen.

WORKS CITED

Primary Sources

Church Meeting Minutes 1808–1854 Tooley Street & Carter Lane. Metropolitan Tabernacle Archives, London.

Church Meeting Minutes 1861–1866 Metropolitan Tabernacle. Metropolitan Tabernacle Archives, London.

Curwen, J. Spencer. *Studies in Worship-Music, Chiefly as Regards Congregational Singing* London: J. Curwen & Sons, 1880.

Elders Minutes 1876–1881 Metropolitan Tabernacle, Metropolitan Tabernacle Archives, London.

Gage, W. L. *Helen on Her Travels: What She Saw and What She Did in Europe*. Hurd & Houghton, New York: 1868.

Gough, John B. *Sunlight and Shadows or Gleanings from My Life Work. Comprising Personal Experiences and Opinions, Anecdotes, Incidents, and Reminiscences, Gathered from Thirty-Seven Years' Experience on the Platform and Among the People at Home and Abroad*. Hartford, CT: A.D. Worthington and Company, 1881.

Metropolitan Tabernacle Archives, London. Baptism Instructions for Elizabeth Broomfield, 17 Feb. 1891.

Spurgeon, C. H. *An All-Round Ministry: Addresses to Ministers and Students*. London: Passmore & Alabaster, 1900.

_____. *The Greatest Fight in the World: Conference Address*. London: Passmore & Alabaster, 1895.

_____. *Lectures to My Students: Addresses Delivered to the Students of the Pastor's College*. Vols. 1–4. London: Passmore & Alabaster, 1881–1894.

_____. *The Lost Sermons of C. H. Spurgeon*. Vols. 1–5 Eds. Christian George, Jason Duesing, and Geoffrey Chang. Nashville: B&H Academic, 2016–2021.

_____. *The Metropolitan Tabernacle: Its History and Work*. Pasadena, TX: Pilgrim Publications, 1990.

_____. *The Metropolitan Tabernacle Pulpit: Sermons Preached and Revised by C. H. Spurgeon*. Vols. 7–63. Pasadena, TX: Pilgrim Publications, 1970–2006.

_____. *The New Park Street Pulpit: Containing Sermons Preached and Revised by the Rev. C. H. Spurgeon, Minister of the Chapel*. Vols. 1–6. Pasadena, TX: Pilgrim Publications, 1975–1991.

_____. *Our Own Hymn-Book: A Collection of Psalms and Hymns for Public, Social, and Private Worship*. London: Passmore & Alabaster, 1885.

_____. *The Pastor in Prayer*. Edinburgh, Banner of Truth, 2004.

_____. *Pictures from Pilgrim's Progress*. Pasadena, TX: Pilgrim Publications, 1992.

_____. *The Salt-Cellars: Being a Collection of Proverbs Together with Homely Notes Thereon*. Vols. 1–2. London: Passmore & Alabaster, 1889–1891.

_____. *The Soul-Winner, or How to Lead Sinners to the Savior*. Pasadena, TX: Pilgrim Publications, 2007.

_____. *Speeches by C.H. Spurgeon at Home and Abroad*. London: Passmore & Alabaster, 1878.

_____. "Spurgeon on Slavery." *The Christian Watchman and Reflector*, January 26, 1860.

_____. *The Sword and the Trowel; A Record of Combat with Sin & Labour for the Lord*. 37 vols. London: Passmore & Alabaster, 1865–1902.

_____. *"Till He Come:" Communion Meditations and Addresses*. Pasadena, TX: Pilgrim, 1971.

_____. *The Treasury of David: Containing an Original Exposition of the Book of Psalms; A Collection of Illustrative Extracts from the Whole Range of Literature; A Series of Homiletical Hints Upon Almost Every Verse; And Lists of Writers Upon Each Psalm*. 7 Vols. London: Passmore & Alabaster, 1869–1885.

Secondary Sources

Bartlett, Edward H. *Mrs. Bartlett and Her Class at the Metropolitan Tabernacle: A Biography by Her Son*. Cannon Beach, OR: Move to Assurance, 2018.

Bebbington, D. W. *Evangelicalism in Modern Britain: A History from the 1730s to the 1980s*. London: Routledge, 2000.

"Letter from Burrage to Mullins." January 3, 1906. The Southern Baptist Theological Seminary Archives.

Carlile, J. C. *C. H. Spurgeon*. Westwood, NJ: Barbour and Company, 1987.

Dallimore, Arnold. *Spurgeon: A New Biography*. Edinburgh: The Banner of Truth Trust, 1999.

Fullerton, W. Y. *Thomas Spurgeon: A Biography*. London: Hodder and Stoughton, 1919.

Fulton, Justin D. *Spurgeon, Our Ally*. Brooklyn, NY: The Pauline Propaganda, 1923.

Johnson, Thomas L. *Twenty-Eight Years a Slave: Or the Story of My Life in Three Continents*. Bournemouth: W. Mate & Sons, Ltd, Printers and Publishers, 1909.

Murray, Iain. *The Forgotten Spurgeon*. Edinburgh: The Banner of Truth Trust, 2002.

Nettles, Tom. *Living by Revealed Truth: The Life and Pastoral Theology of Charles Haddon Spurgeon*. Ross-shire: Christian Focus, 2013.

Paine, Albert Bigelow. *Mark Twain, a Biography: The Personal and Literary Life of Samuel Langhorne Clemens*. United Kingdom: Harper & Brothers, 1912.

Williams, W. *Personal Reminiscences of Charles Haddon Spurgeon*. London: The Religious Tract Society, 1895.